Feed Your Cells!

7 Ways to Make Health Food Fast, Easy, *And Gluten Free*

by

Andrea Purcell, NMD

DEDICATION

This book is dedicated to all of my patients who have come to me for integrated, natural health care. Thank you for entrusting me with your health and inspiring me to ask questions, do more, learn more, and become more. With much love, peace, and gratitude, I honor you!

COPYRIGHT NOTICE

ACKNOWLEDGMENTS

This book, like everything else in my life, has been birthed out of the ability to see a need and uncover the truth behind it.

This book is not the end of anything; it is just the beginning for you, for me, and for all of the patients who have helped me understand the difficulties of preparing healthy food in our fast-paced lives.

Having lived on both coasts, I can no longer deny that life is busy. What coast you are on determines the kind of busy. Nevertheless, I assure you the pace is the same. East Coasters have more rigid schedules and set timetables, while West Coasters work just as hard but on their own schedules, molding their days to fit their own calendars, not others'. Working with my patients on both coasts has taught me the tremendous need for a way to prepare fast and healthy food at home.

A few family friends once told me that before I was a toddler, my mother was blending up spinach and broccoli and putting them in my baby bottle. It seems almost normal to do now, but a lot of things have changed in the last forty years. I remember that when I went places as a kid, my mom would always pack our lunch from home because, in her words, "I don't want us eating any junk," and "We can certainly eat better with food cooked from home than with anything else that could be bought outside the house." This point was driven home one day when after hours of whining for a hotdog at Madison Square Garden, she finally acquiesced and bought one for me. Within hours, I was nauseous, and by the time we returned home, I promptly vomited all over the place. I was sick to my stomach with food poisoning! My understanding about the importance of nutrition and avoidance of processed foods started at home, and for that, I am eternally grateful.

Many thanks to you, Mom!

Additionally, I want to thank all of my patients who have come to me for natural, integrated health care and have taught me so much in the process. It has been a mutually rewarding journey of learning and healing.

Along those lines, the naturopathic profession has been a true calling for me, and it has allowed me to realize my higher purpose. That purpose is to leave a legacy of a new health paradigm—a health paradigm that leaves an integrated and holistic platform for the next generation to view medicine and health from.

ADVANCED PRAISE & RAVE REVIEWS

"What Dr. Purcell has done is spectacular. I just received my copy of the recipe book you hold in your hand, and I cannot believe how straightforward and informative it is. With this sort of guidance and encouragement, healthy eating and preparation seems within reach. I urge you to put this recipe book to good use! The cover alone is unbelievable and speaks volumes." ~ *Dr. Samantha Slotnick, O.D., F.A.A.O., F.C.O.V.D.*

"The Raw Cereal Blend is delicious and so satisfying! It took a while to prepare because we had to roast our own hazelnuts (couldn't find them already roasted), and we doubled up on the currants because we couldn't find dried cranberries without sugar." ~ *K.P., La Palma, CA*

"Bought the cookbook, and highly recommend it. Love the recipes!" ~ *E.R., Huntington Beach, CA*

"Received my book on Friday, and made my first recipe. Yummmm!" ~ *D. H-B., Long Beach, CA*

"Feeding my cells with Banana Blue Muffins. Great recipe. Thanks!" ~ *S.T., Orange County, CA*

"The sweet potato fries are my new favorite!" ~ *D.S., Placentia, CA*

"Just wanted you to know that we love the cookbook! Especially the desserts. The cookies were a hit even though I forgot the applesauce. Mike is enjoying the almond butter bites. Alexandria can't have nuts yet so I used sunflower butter instead. Delish. I brought the pie to a party today, and it too was a big success. We also have been making double batches of the carrot ginger dressing for salads. Now in all seriousness, your book inspired me to get back to very basic, simple meals and eliminate as many processed foods as possible, as well as reduce refined flours, sugars, and cut out dairy again since I have a sensitivity. We have been eating 'clean' for 2 weeks. Mike has lost 6 lbs., and my skin has cleared up. I have a ton of energy, and feel great! Alexandria loved the swiss chard egg scramble too!" ~ *R.Z., Katonah, NY*

"Yesterday we made the Oatmeal Harvest Cookies from your *Feed Your Cells!* cookbook, and our kids love them! They were easy to make, and they were excited that there could actually be a cookie made from healthy ingredients. This will become a staple in our cupboard. Thanks for the great recipe!" ~ *B.L., Ojai, CA*

"Setting up my week, turkey chili came out great. Rockin' the salsa in the background." ~ *S.S.*

TABLE OF CONTENTS

Resources

About the Author

INTRODUCTION

My patients ask me year after year to recommend cookbooks so that they can have some variety and direction in the land of healthy eating. Ugh! How frustrating for me! My dilemma is multifaceted:

- **Vegetarian cookbooks** are too high in refined carbohydrates;
- **Cookbooks for diabetics** use dairy and artificial sweeteners;
- **Healthy cookbooks** often times use too many, and even "strange" ingredients, which leave people overwhelmed;
- **Cookbooks focused on "good tasting food"** are frequently very unhealthy.

Everyone seems to have a different definition of what good food is. My definition of good food is that it should taste good and be good for us. I have a few goals with this book:

- ✓ **Goal 1** – to help you realize that eating healthy is not as time-consuming as you may think;
- ✓ **Goal 2** – to show you that taste and flavor do not have to be sacrificed to eat healthfully;
- ✓ **Goal 3** – to show you ways to enable you to make healthy cooking and eating part of your lifestyle, day in and day out, week after week.

With some forethought, a delicious meal can be prepared with minimal effort and huge nutritious impact. Believe it or not, I find chopping vegetables to be relaxing. If you are unable to find the Zen in chopping vegetables, have your spouse or kids do it. Involving the whole family in making healthy eating fun will make your journey much easier.

TRUTH #1 – Eating healthy is necessary in order to promote and maintain optimal body function. I view food similarly to the way our cars need gasoline. If we put watered down gas in our car, we're going to get sub-optimal performance. High quality food is our gasoline — it keeps our systems running cleanly and efficiently. Each day, our health is affected by our food choices, positively or negatively. We may not notice on a day-to-day basis, but we do month after month or year after year. Just like our cars, our bodies have the ability to perform optimally when given the proper building blocks. Good, clean food provides those building blocks. Food is the foundation of health and a healthy lifestyle. Feed your body well, and it will run optimally for years to come!

TRUTH #2 – Life is busy. Food choices that we make every day either lead us closer to health or to disease. You simply cannot compromise the gift of health by making poor food choices due to time constraints.

What I have found with many of my patients is that people need ideas on how to prepare healthy food that tastes great in a short amount of time. This book is for you.

THE PAYOFF

Eating healthy makes you feel better — that means more energy, more focus, and more performance from your body each day. When you eat cleanly, there is less toxin buildup, less fat storage, less strain on your organ systems, higher nutrient absorption, and better performance. It's that simple.

Sometimes, it's helpful to think of bodies being like filters. Everything that you breathe, eat, drink, and place on your skin, your body needs to filter. Over time, the filters start to get clogged and gunk starts to accumulate. This leads to feeling unwell. When you eat fresh, whole foods from nature, there is less that your system needs to filter.

The foods and recipes listed in this book will run clean through the engines of your body. Food enters. It is utilized. Energy is created, and waste is eliminated. It is a highly efficient process.

I love the concept that people are regenerative instead of degenerative. Good, whole food keeps your billions of cells fed and nourished to perform the thousands of necessary bodily processes each day. Food helps you to regenerate. Making a choice to eat healthfully, one day at a time, is making a huge step towards wellness.

Multiple times every day, you feed yourself. What are you really doing? You are feeding your cells. Just take a minute and think about that the next time you reach for the chocolate croissant. Ask yourself, "Can my cells really create energy from this? Is this what my body needs to prevent arthritis and disease?" You already know the answer to that question.

The way I see it, most people fall into one of two categories:

❶ **People who really don't know how to choose, cook, and prepare healthy food**; (When these people don't have the knowledge, they cannot choose correctly. Most people rely on precooked, packaged, or fast foods.)

❷ People who know how to feed themselves, but they don't because of feeling tired, depressed, overwhelmed, or just too busy. (These people know what to do, but they don't. So, instead, they, too, rely on prepackaged convenience foods or they skip meals.)

This book is for both types of people. This book will teach you simple, healthy ways of cooking, and the recipes are short and sweet.

I would like to think that you will never consider a drive-through again when you have one of these meals in your lunch box in the passenger seat.

The recipes I have chosen are simple and easy. Even without any kitchen knowledge, you should be able to follow along and be successful. The key to feeding yourself well is preparation. Knowing the day or night before what the following day requires will keep you one step ahead and properly fed. I encourage my patients to prepare big pots or bowls of certain items that will get them through two to three days. Generally, Sundays and Wednesdays are good food preparation days because they will move you through your week. In this way, you can maximize your time in the kitchen. With certain recipes, I almost always make a double batch, and often, it is just as easy to make two as it is to make one. A good rule of thumb is to always have dinner leftovers to be eaten for lunch the next day.

This book is focused on real, whole food — food that is from nature and contains single ingredients. None of the food mentioned is prepackaged or processed. This food generally comes from the produce section, the butcher, the fish market, and the local health food store. Many of these items can be purchased at Trader Joes® or Whole Foods® if there is one in your area.

If you have the ability to put a few cooking herbs in a pot and grow them in a sunny window, you will have access to fresh herbs at any time. These will add a lot of flavor to your dishes. I recommend fresh thyme, rosemary, oregano, tarragon, dill, and basil.

May you share these recipes with your family and the people you love, and may they get excited about cooking and feeding themselves food that promotes good health and a long life.

Bon Appétit!

Dr. Andrea Purcell

Dr. Andrea Purcell

CHAPTER 1
A Healthy Kitchen

What constitutes a healthy kitchen?

A healthy kitchen is defined as a room in the house that contains the basic building blocks for creating healthy meals. It does not contain any of the following:

artificial sweeteners; processed foods; prepackaged foods; processed frozen foods; refined breads, grains, or baked goods; white sugar; or unhealthy snacks.

A kitchen should be used for nourishment of our bodies and minds. It should not contain food items that are inflammatory and promote disease.

Many people do not know how important their health is until they lose it. Then they realize that no amount of money, no job, and no vacation can ever be earned, accomplished, or enjoyed without good health.

Once you lose your health, you can lose everything!

Food choices that you make every day either lead you closer to health or to disease.

People will tell me, "I don't have the time to cook or prepare food." My response is this: for everything in life, there is a trade-off. It is of no use to gain wealth but lose health simultaneously due to overwork. Choosing to eat well every day brings you closer to health.

To assist you in creating a healthy kitchen, I have listed the items in mine. Additionally, I feel so strongly about nutrition and good health that I have created this cookbook with your busy schedules and health in mind!

MY FRIDGE

When you take a close look at the items inside my refrigerator, you will notice that I do not have many sauces, salad dressings, dips, or other items in bottles, jars, or containers. Generally speaking, these items are filled with fat and sugar, and they tend to be processed. These items are unnecessary and just take up space.

Depending on the day of the week, I may have more or fewer vegetables, but they are the mainstays inside my refrigerator. With these items, I can whip up a great salad, add spice and flavor to dressings, steam vegetables, or make a fresh juice. The goal by the end of each week is to eat all the vegetables so that the fridge is empty and ready for a refill of fresh produce. I try to alternate the vegetables each week so that I don't get in a rut and buy the same items all the time. Remember, variety is the spice of life!

- ◆ Unsweetened Almond Milk
- ◆ Apples
- ◆ Juicing Ingredients (Carrots, Swiss Chard, Celery and Cucumber)
- ◆ Salad Greens (Arugula, Spinach or Romaine Lettuce)
- ◆ Zucchini
- ◆ Broccoli
- ◆ Parsley
- ◆ Cilantro
- ◆ Pickles
- ◆ Olives
- ◆ Hot Sauce
- ◆ Parmesan Cheese
- ◆ Spicy brown mustard
- ◆ Boysenberry Preserves
- ◆ Tejava (Unsweetened Black Tea)
- ◆ Pure Maple Syrup

- Organic Butter
- Organic Eggs
- Coconut Water with Aloe Pieces
- Braggs® Amino Acids
- Organic Ketchup

COOKING BASKET

This originally was a fruit basket that I kept on the counter, but I needed the counter space, so I hung it from the ceiling. Depending on the week, it can contain the following:

- Onions (2 to 6 small, yellow or brown)
- Garlic (2 bulbs)
- Ginger (1 palm-size piece)
- Avocados
- Pears
- Lemons or Limes
- Oranges
- Sweet potatoes or white potatoes
- Tomatoes

FREEZER

- Grass-fed ground beef
- Organic chicken breast
- Peas
- Blueberries, Strawberries or Bananas
- Organic Butter
- Spinach
- Edamame

- Turbot Fish Fillets
- Homemade Seventeen-Bean Soup
- Almond Butter Bites (The recipe can be found later in this book.)
- Organic Coffee

SPICE SHELF

- Cinnamon (Ground And Sticks)
- Sea Salt and Truffle Salt
- Dried Garlic and Herb Blend
- Dried Italian Spices
- Dried Basil, Dill and Oregano
- Crushed Red Pepper (Cayenne)
- Onion Powder and Flakes
- Dried Cumin and Cardamom
- Nutmeg
- Pumpkin Pie Spice
- Extra Virgin Olive Oil (EVOO) and Grape Seed Oil
- Bragg's Apple Cider Vinegar
- Agave Syrup
- Flavored Liquid Stevia (4 Types)
- Cocoa Powder (Unsweetened)

DRY GOODS

- Gluten-Free Oats
- Raw Almonds (Whole and Slivered)
- Chopped Walnuts and Pecans
- Raw Sunflower Seeds Pumpkin Seeds and Pine Nuts
- Dried Raisins, Currants and Cranberries

◆ Whole Golden Flaxseeds
◆ Garbanzo, Brown Rice and Almond Meal (These are used as alternatives to flour.)
◆ Quinoa, Wild Rice, Lentils, Brown Rice and Corn Meal
◆ Cornstarch, Baking Powder and Baking Soda
◆ Almond Butter
◆ Rice Cakes
◆ Dried Coconut (Unsweetened)
◆ Rice Crackers
◆ Wheat-Free and Dairy-Free Pancake Mix
◆ Bagged or Loose Tea (Black, Green and Herbal Varieties)
◆ Mineral Water

Gluten Free

CHAPTER 2
Gluten-Free

The latest conversation among patients, consumers, doctors, and nutritionists is whether or not to be gluten-free. Does it have any health benefits? Is it better for you and your family? Can it help with digestive symptoms? Is it a good idea in general?

The information about gluten and the awareness around Celiac disease seems to have thrown the nation into a gluten-free frenzy. Many people are eating gluten-free as a type of fad diet. They have heard that gluten is bad and have chosen to avoid it as a way to be healthy. As the awareness builds so does the availability of gluten-free products. It is easier than ever to find gluten-free breads, cakes, cookies, and brownie mixes. Buyer beware, gluten-free eating is not necessarily synonymous with healthy eating.

This chapter will cover the who, what, where, when, and why to going gluten-free and what exactly is gluten and where is it found?

Gluten is found in the protein component of some grains. Not all grains contain gluten. Examples of foods that include grains are: bread, pasta, tortillas, cereal, baked goods and cookies. Gluten is what makes bread moist and stick together.

The grains to avoid when you are avoiding gluten are wheat, rye, barley, spelt, and possibly oats. Oats can be grown in fields close to wheat and other grains that contain gluten and may become cross contaminated with them. Oats have a protein that looks similar to gluten. It is not gluten, but in a person with a weakened digestive system the body may react to oats as well. Due to these two factors, oats may or may not cause a reaction and a sensitive patient is best to use gluten-free oats or avoid them all together.

There are two main proteins in gluten; gliadins and glutenins. Gliadin, found in wheat, is what leads to Celiac disease and gluten sensitivity. Barley and rye contain a gliadin that looks very similar to the one in wheat, and therefore, when the body reacts to wheat gluten, it usually reacts to barley and rye gluten too.

CELIAC DISEASE

The shocking news in 2003 was that 1 in 133 people had Celiac disease. The statistics show that Celiac disease is much more prevalent than the conventional medical community acknowledged it to be.

What is Celiac disease?

Celiac disease is a genetic intolerance to gluten contained in wheat, rye, spelt, and barley. The allergy to gluten damages the absorptive capability of the small intestine leading to mal-absorption. When people have Celiac disease they are unable to absorb vitamins, minerals, and nutrients properly leading to severe depletion.

Depending on the degree of mal-absorption, the signs and symptoms of Celiac disease vary among individuals, ranging from no symptoms to many. All body functions and organs rely on nutrients absorbed through the digestive tract for proper function. Severe depletion over time can lead to total body breakdown and will literally affect every organ system. There are no drugs available to treat Celiac disease and the current recommendation is the avoidance of any and all gluten.

Once considered rare, Celiac disease, is now a common autoimmune disease afflicting one in 133 people according to the National Institutes of Health. Since Celiac disease is genetic, if you or a loved one has Celiac disease there is a good chance that first and second-degree relatives will have the diagnosis as well. Currently 97% of Americans with Celiac disease are not diagnosed, and 500,000 new cases are expected to be diagnosed in 2012, due to increased public awareness.

Celiac disease is diagnosed via a blood test called Tissue Trans Glutaminase (TTG) IgM & IgA, as well as through a biopsy of the gastrointestinal tract. In order to be properly diagnosed, gluten must be consumed in the diet for 4-6 weeks before and during testing.

As a medical necessity, there are three groups of people who should avoid gluten:

- Any person with a diagnosis of Celiac disease.
- Any person with an allergic reaction to wheat as determined either by an IgG blood or an IgE blood or skin scratch test test.
- Any person with gluten sensitivity- People can be sensitive to gluten without having Celiac disease.

THE CELIAC ICEBERG

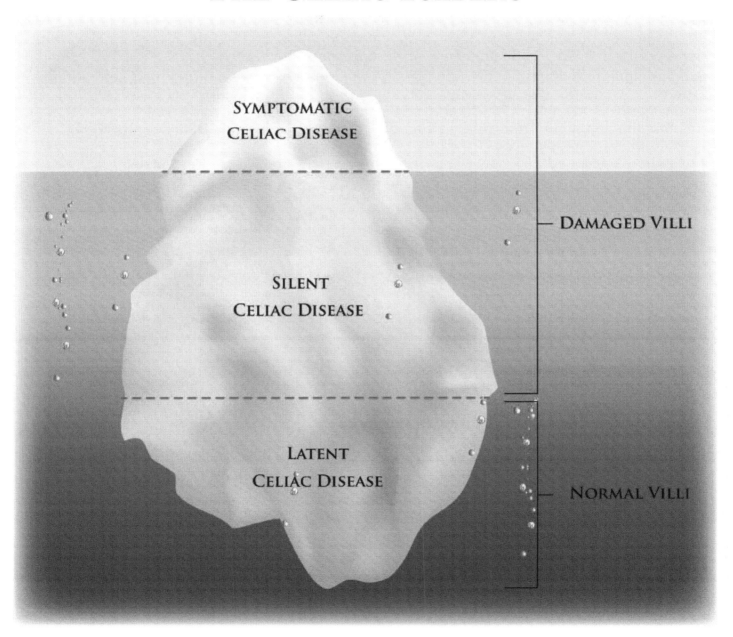

GLUTEN SENSITIVITY vs. ALLERGY

Many people are sensitive to wheat and/or gluten but do not have the diagnosis of Celiac disease. Sensitivities can cause symptoms such as skin reactions, congestion in the throat, ears, or sinuses, digestive upset, or other body inflammation such as fatigue and aching joints.

If someone is sensitive, the test results will be negative but the patient generally feels better when they avoid gluten. People can become sensitive to foods after repeatedly eating them over a long time, or from a slow breakdown of the digestive lining due to environmental exposures to toxins, medications and vaccinations.

ALLERGY/SENSTITIVITY SYMPTOMS INCLUDE:

- Fatigue or Low Energy
- Irritability, Mood Swings and/or Anxiety
- Eczema, Dry Skin or Other Dermatitis (Rash)
- Inability To Lose or Gain Weight
- Insomnia or Restless Sleep
- Recurrent Infections (Sinus, Respiratory, Vaginal, Urinary)
- Organ Pain (Kidney/Liver)
- Diarrhea and/or Constipation
- Chronic Anemia
- Reflux (Gerd)

GLUTEN – HIDDEN FOODS:

- Dijon Mustard
- Soups and Broths
- Rice Milk
- Shampoo/Conditioner
- Dextrin
- Sliced Deli Meats
- Soy Sauce
- Skin Cream/Moisturizers
- Combination Spices
- Cheese Spread
- Licking Envelopes
- Compounded (Hormone) Creams

AT HOME TEST

A simple test can be done at home to determine if a person is sensitive to gluten. Avoid all gluten for 14 days. This means all gluten. Read labels carefully because many items contain hidden gluten such as cereals, sliced deli meats, and canned soups. After 14 days reintroduce foods containing gluten 1-2x daily for three days in a row. Observe the body for any signs of gluten sensitivity that are listed on the previous page.

Why is Gluten allergy/sensitivity so prevalent today?

A recent study posted in the Annals of Medicine in 2010 found that people could lose their tolerance to gluten as they age. These people are not born with the genetic intolerance commonly seen with Celiac disease but are developing the intolerance later on in life. This suggests a weakening of digestive function due to repeated exposure to gluten and other food allergens, which can cause a slow breakdown of the digestive lining known as "leaky gut"; other culprits are: toxin exposure; antibiotics; medications; and even vaccines.

It is well known that certain medications can weaken and even damage digestive function. Just released in February 2011 in the Journal of Nature, a study, linked Accutane, a drug used to treat acne, to an increase in Celiac disease and inflammatory bowel disorders.

Scientists state that the active component in the drug can exacerbate the presentation of Celiac disease in patients who were mild enough cases to be asymptomatic prior to taking the drug. Plaintiffs have won more than $45 million in compensation for Accutane side effects, such as ulcerative colitis and Crohn's disease.

What does it mean to be gluten-free?

Eating and cooking gluten-free means consuming a whole food diet devoid of grains containing gluten.

Don't be fooled by gluten-free marketing; not everything gluten-free is in your best interest.

Often, eating processed and refined grains that do not contain gluten, such as rice, potato, and tapioca flours can still be high in simple carbohydrates, low in fiber, and are often combined with unhealthy sugars and oils. Eating gluten-free, this way, is not healthy at all, and weight gain can result due to excess intake of carbohydrates. Gluten-free pizza crust, cookies, crackers, muffins, breads, cake mixes, pastas and cereals are all refined, and although they don't contain gluten, they are not healthy when consumed in moderate to large amounts. These can cause blood sugar irregularities that result in feeling emotionally unstable and anxious. **The key to a healthy diet is eating a well-balanced whole food or plant based diet that is gluten-free.**

HOW TO COOK GLUTEN-FREE

For those first diagnosed with Celiac disease, the act of cooking and eating initially becomes very stressful. Learning a few tried and true simple recipes that can be whipped up in a flash will be extremely helpful. Cooking gluten-free is much easier than baking gluten-free. My initial recommendation is that a person start with cooking.

The first thing to do is to focus on a plant based diet. This includes all vegetables, fruits, nuts, seeds, lean proteins, protein powders from whey, rice, soy, or pea, and dairy products in moderation. These foods will become the foundation of a daily food plan.

Remember that gluten is only found in grains so you will need to know your list of safe grains.

Experiment with non-gluten grains and find some easy recipes that include acceptable items such as brown rice, wild rice, quinoa, amaranth, buckwheat, sorghum, and teff.

There are many benefits to home cooking. You have complete control over what you eat and the quality of ingredients, plus there will always be leftovers for lunch the next day; " hooray"!

WHERE TO BEGIN

Now that you know the basics, you are armed with information to successfully eat gluten-free. Here are five health tips to follow if you decide to eliminate gluten:

✓ **Keep it simple.**

Eat foods in their most natural state such as: fruits, vegetables, beans, hormone free organic meats, nuts and eggs.

✓ **Buy 1-2 healthy gluten-free cookbooks.**

These will help you prepare meals and baked goods that everyone can enjoy.

✓ **Just because it is gluten-free doesn't mean that it's healthy.**

Many processed gluten-free foods contain refined grains, sugars, and unhealthy oils. These can cause blood sugars to rise and are lacking in vitamins and minerals.

✓ **Know your safe grains.**

Safe grains include: rice, corn, and quinoa. Quinoa is actually a seed.

✓ **Be a super label reader.**

Wheat and gluten are hidden in many items as fillers. Check your tomato sauces, soups, seasonings, chicken broth, soy sauce, and most baked goods.

REFERENCES:

Fasano A, Berti I, Gerarduzzi T, et al. Prevalence of Celiac disease in at-risk and not-at-risk groups in the United States. Archives of Internal Medicine. 2003;163(3):268–292.
R. W. DePaolo, V. Abadie, F. Tang, H. Fehlner-Peach, J. A. Hall, + et al
Co-adjuvant effects of retinoic acid and IL-15 induce inflammatory immunity to dietary antigens
Nature 471, 220-224 doi:10.1038/
Carlo Catassi1,2, Debby Kryszak1, Bushra Bhatti1, Craig Sturgeon1, Kathy Helzlsouer3, Sandra L. Clipp3, Daniel Gelfond4, Elaine Puppa1, Anthony Sferruzza5 & Alessio Fasano1
"Natural History of Celiac Disease Autoimmunity in a USA Cohort Followed Since1974"
Annals of Medicine: October 2010, Vol. 42, No. 7 , Pages 530-538

THIS ISN'T JUST ANOTHER COOKBOOK

This isn't just another cookbook, or a "how to guide" to cook gluten-free. It is much more than that. This is a guide to healthy eating that is gluten-free. This book is geared towards everyday people who want to use food to prevent disease.

The focus is foods that are nourishing and anti-inflammatory. The goal is to help feed yourself at a cellular level.

The recipes contained in this book are purposely low in sugar. Sugar lowers our immune system, is inflammatory, and feeds cancer cells. People who are focused on preventing and surviving cancer must reduce sugars in their diets. Take a look at some of the diseases caused by inflammation; arthritis, heart disease, cancer, autoimmune conditions, fibromyalgia, skin complaints, and dementia.

We have the power to control the level of inflammation inside our bodies. We can do this by making the right food choices. Every item we place in our bodies should be used as a building block to create energy; only real food can do this. Our bodies contain the exact same elements as those found in real food that balances and nourishes us.

Chemicals in fake foods create imbalances, which damage our cells leading to accelerated aging, and body degeneration. Fake, processed foods are harmful because they damage our cells.

Our bodies have this amazing ability to heal themselves, and I guarantee that every reader has experienced it first hand. When we break a bone, we set it; or if we get a paper cut we put some Neosporin on it to make sure it doesn't get infected. What are we really doing? We are putting the bone back in the correct place, washing off the finger, and we are waiting for the body to heal.

There is no magic medicine that causes the bone or the wound to heal; we wait for the body to perform its own magic. So when we feed our cells, we help that internal magic along. Eating fresh unprocessed food (Food that grows) reduces the chances of developing body inflammation that leads to disease. This is all about you living a great life!

Eating properly and following the guidelines in this book can make a difference in your life and the lives of people you love. Following this simple guide to healthy eating provides essential nutrition at the cellular level, while decreasing inflammation, and promoting proper body balance.

The famous quote of Benjamin Franklin couldn't be truer today:

"An ounce of prevention really is worth a pound of cure."

This is where natural medicine shines. Get focused on feeding your cells! Your body will be so happy it will keep on functioning for many healthy years to come.

VEGETABLE SPOTLIGHT!

"KALE"

The King of the cruciferous vegetable empire! I encourage you to experiment with kale, and incorporate it in into your weekly shopping list.

When you see this vegetable you should be thinking detoxification and cancer protection.

It is high in vitamins: A, C, and K.

Researchers can now identify over 45 different flavonoids or phytochemicals in kale, which assist our liver in detoxifying cancer-causing chemicals from the environment. Kale's cancer-preventive benefits have been clearly linked to its unusual concentration of two types of antioxidants, namely, carotenoids and flavonoids.

Kale has proven risk-lowering benefits for bladder, breast, colon, ovarian and prostate cancer.

Specifically, kale's nutrient richness stands out in three particular areas:

(1) High in antioxidants;

(2) Anti-inflammatory compounds;

(3) Anti-cancer compounds.

CREAMY KALE SALAD

Here's a great kale salad recipe for you to enjoy.

Ingredients:

1 ripe avocado, halved

2 Tablespoons apple cider vinegar

2 teaspoons spicy brown mustard

3 Tablespoons grape seed oil

½ bunch kale, stemmed and coarsely chopped

1 small red beet, grated

1 apple, chopped into bite size pieces

⅓ cup toasted pecans, chopped

Sea salt and pepper to taste

Directions:

To make dressing: Combine avocado, grape seed oil, vinegar and mustard in food processor, sprinkle with salt and pepper. This will be thick. Add 2 Tablespoons of water if needed.

In a bowl combine apple pieces, kale, beets, and pecans. Pour dressing on top and toss, add sea salt as desired.

Makes 4 servings.

KALE SHAKE

A great shake in the morning or after a workout.

Ingredients:

1 cup coconut milk, unsweetened
4-5 kale leaves, chopped
5 frozen strawberries
½ banana
Pinch cinnamon
2-5 drops liquid stevia, vanilla flavored

Directions:

Add coconut milk and kale leaves to blender, blend until creamy, add strawberries and banana blend until pureed; then add cinnamon and stevia, blend and drink!

Makes 1 serving.

CRISPY KALE CHIPS

Ingredients:

1 (12 oz.) bunch of washed curly kale (Chop off thick stems at end, and then chop each leaf into 4 pieces.)
2 Tablespoons EVOO
1 Tablespoon lemon juice
½ teaspoon sea salt / truffle salt

Directions:

Place all chopped kale in a bowl.
Toss with EVOO, lemon juice.
Spread out on cookie sheet.
Sprinkle with sea salt.
Bake in oven for 30 minutes until crispy.

Makes 4 servings.

CHAPTER 3
Healthy Breakfasts

There's an old adage that goes like this:

"Eat like a king for breakfast, a prince for lunch, and a pauper for dinner."

The typical American schedule is just the opposite. In fact, one of the questions I ask my patients is, "Are you a breakfast person?" Many people do not eat breakfast or eat a very poor rendition of it. Starting your day with simple carbohydrates and sugar is appetite stimulating and sets you up for overconsumption for the rest of the day. In order not to blow it at the starting gate, my breakfast recommendations are packed with nutrition and, best of all, they are easy!

Starting your day with protein, vegetables, and phytonutrients that come from fruits and vegetables is incredibly important. It gets the fires of metabolism revved and maintains your energy throughout the morning.

If you are short on time, many of these items can be chopped and prepared the night before so that all it takes is a little combining in the morning. If you are just not hungry in the morning, take it to go and eat it at 10:00 AM. All of these are better choices than grabbing something on the go that is less healthy simply because you are starving.

As a reminder, there are three recipes in this section that call for oats. If you are sensitive to gluten or have Celiac disease then you must choose gluten-free oats. Oats can sometimes be contaminated with gluten depending on where they are grown.

BANANA-BLUE BREAKFAST MUFFINS

This gluten-free and dairy-free recipe is a keeper! Start your day with this high fiber and antioxidant rich breakfast delight. This batter can be made with or without a food processor, and it can sit pre-mixed in the fridge for up to four days. Once made, muffins can be frozen for future use. Need I say more?

Ingredients:

1 cup gluten-free oats or oat bran
1 cup almond milk
¼ cup flaxseed meal or ground flaxseed
4 medium-sized bananas
¾ cup blueberries fresh or frozen
½ cup and 2 Tablespoons agave syrup
10 drops vanilla-flavored liquid stevia
1 large egg
¼ cup grapeseed or canola oil
¾ cup rice flour
¾ cup almond meal, or garbanzo or fava flour
1 teaspoon baking powder
½ teaspoon baking soda
½ teaspoon cinnamon, ground
¼ teaspoon nutmeg, ground
¼ teaspoon salt

Directions:

Preheat your oven to 350°F.

Place gluten-free oats, almond milk, and flaxseed in a bowl or food processor. Mix or pulse to combine. Let mixture stand for 15 minutes or until the oat bran and flaxseed have absorbed the milk.

Coat a 12 cup muffin pan with cooking spray or use muffin papers.

Add 4 ripe bananas to the oat bran and flaxseed mixture and mix until smooth. Add agave, stevia, egg, and oil and mix until smooth.

Whisk together rice flour, almond meal, baking powder, baking soda, cinnamon, nutmeg, and salt in a bowl. Add to cereal mixture in bowl or food processor and mix until smooth. Stir in blueberries.

Fill each muffin cup with ½ cup of batter. Bake 20 to 25 minutes or until muffin tops are browned and a toothpick inserted comes out clean.

Cool on wire racks.

Makes 12 to 15 muffins.

HEALTHY HOT CEREAL

Since quinoa is a complete protein, it provides excellent morning nourishment. For a bit more of a protein punch, add half a scoop of your favorite protein powder to the cooked quinoa before it leaves the pot. Since variety is the spice of life I almost always add three or more toppings.

Ingredients:

¾ cup water
½ cup quinoa flakes
¼ cup unsweetened rice milk

Choose your toppings:

1 Tablespoon raisins or dried cranberries
1 Tablespoon fresh apple, chopped
1 Tablespoon chopped nuts or sunflower seeds
1 Tablespoon dried, unsweetened coconut
1 Tablespoon ground flaxseeds
Liquid vanilla-flavored stevia to taste

Directions:

Bring ¾ cup of water to boil and stir in quinoa flakes. Cover, reduce heat, and simmer for up to 5 minutes or until all liquid is absorbed. Turn off heat.

Pour cooked quinoa into a bowl, add 2 drops liquid stevia and rice milk, and mix well. Choose your toppings and sprinkle them on top or mix in — it's your choice!

Makes 1 serving.

RAW CEREAL BLEND

So many patients ask me about cereal. In my opinion, cereal is a fast food. It is processed, high in carbohydrates, low in protein, and often contains refined sugars. Overall, it is just a horrible way to start your day.

Here is my suggestion for a healthier cereal. Most people don't know that rolled oats can be eaten raw, and they are quite tasty!

Ingredients:

½ cup sunflower seeds
¼ cup pumpkin seeds
2 Tablespoons slivered almonds
4 cups gluten free rolled oats or quinoa flakes
⅓ cup ground flax seeds
¼ cup currants
¼ cup dried cranberries
1 cup roasted hazelnuts, chopped

Directions:

Put the sunflower and pumpkin seeds in a dry frying pan and cook over medium heat for 3 minutes until golden, tossing the seeds regularly to prevent them from burning. Let cool.

Mix all ingredients in a large bowl until thoroughly combined. Store mixture in an airtight container in the fridge for up to 2 weeks at a time.

When you want cereal, scoop out a ½ cup, add to a bowl, and add your milk of choice. It's easy, nutritious, and good!

Makes 12 servings.

EASY QUINOA HASH

Remember to eat like a king for breakfast! Quinoa has the protein and nutrients for lasting energy. As long as you have some cooked quinoa ready, this dish is a cinch! It can be mixed with feta, turkey, eggs, hummus, zucchini, or roasted cubed root vegetables for any breakfast, lunch, or dinner combination.

Ingredients:

2 Tablespoons EVOO
3 Tablespoons onion, finely chopped
1 cup cooked quinoa
3 Tablespoons pecans, finely chopped
¼ teaspoon ground thyme
1 pinch of sea salt
1 to 2 teaspoon(s) fresh herbs of your choice (e.g. parsley, cilantro, sage, basil, etc.), chopped

Directions:

Heat onion in a skillet on medium heat and sauté for 30 seconds. Add quinoa, pecans, and thyme, and spread everything evenly across your skillet and cook for 45 seconds without stirring. Then, stir and sauté for 2 to 3 minutes until golden brown.

Remove from heat, add salt and herbs, and enjoy!

Makes 1 serving.

EGG SCRAMBLE WITH SWISS CHARD AND GARLIC

Start your day with protein and veggies! This dish is so satisfying! Sweet potatoes are high in vitamin A, and fiber when you keep the skin on. Swiss chard has thirteen antioxidants, and it is second only to spinach as one of the world's most nutrient-dense vegetables. High in vitamins A, C, and K, it is a mild green that comes on a large stalk. I recommend coring out the thicker stalk portion and then chopping it as instructed below.

The recipe also calls for roasted garlic. If you don't have roasted garlic, you can always slice fresh garlic, sauté it in one teaspoon of EVOO for three to four minutes, and then add as directed.

Ingredients:

1 large sweet potato
1 teaspoon butter
4 eggs, lightly beaten
4 cloves roasted garlic, thinly sliced
½ cup swiss chard, stemmed and chopped
¼ cup crumbled goat cheese

Directions:

Preheat broiler.

Gently boil whole potato (skin on) until tender. Drain. When cool enough to handle, cut into quarter-inch cubes.

Melt butter in a 10-inch cast-iron skillet or an oven-proof sauté pan. Turn heat to medium-low and add potatoes. Cook slowly until golden brown (about 10 minutes) and season with salt.

Move potatoes in a pile to one side of skillet. Pour eggs into other side and lightly scramble. When eggs are not quite fully cooked, add garlic and swiss chard and fold together with potatoes. Season to taste, top with goat cheese, and lightly brown under broiler.

Makes 2 servings.

TOFU SCRAMBLE

This is a vegetarian breakfast option that is high in protein and so simple!

Ingredients:

½ cup brown onion, chopped
½ stalk celery, diced
1 tub extra firm tofu, drained and cubed or crumbled
1 pinch black pepper
½ teaspoon turmeric, cumin, or chili powder
½ cup carrots, red pepper, or snap peas, diced
½ cup fresh parsley, chopped
1 teaspoon sea salt
1 to 2 teaspoon(s) EVOO

Directions:

Heat oil in a frying pan, and add carrots, celery, and onion, cook until soft (about 5 to 7 minutes). Add parsley, turmeric, salt, and pepper. Add tofu and stir-fry for about 5 minutes.

Makes 2 servings.

COLORFUL HASHBROWNS

Make this on a Sunday morning or the night before. Either way, once it is made, it can easily be combined with eggs or chicken sausage for a hearty and delicious breakfast. You can cheat by buying the butternut squash and sweet potato already peeled and diced.

Ingredients:

1 medium celery root, diced into quarter-inch pieces
1 large carrot, diced into quarter-inch pieces
1 large parsnip, diced into quarter-inch pieces
1 medium butternut squash, peeled and cubed into quarter-inch pieces
1 medium sweet potato or white potato, diced into 1-inch pieces
1 medium onion, chopped
2 garlic cloves, minced
2 Tablespoons flat leaf parsley, chopped
6 fresh sage leaves
⅓ cup EVOO
Sea salt and pepper to taste

Directions:

Preheat oven to 400°F.

On one cookie sheet, spread the celery, parsnip, and carrot, and toss with 1 to 2 Tablespoons of EVOO. On another cookie sheet, spread the butternut squash and the potato, and toss and coat with 1 to 2 Tablespoons EVOO. Place both sheets in the oven and roast. Stir after 15 minutes. Once vegetables are tender and browned, remove from the oven.

In a skillet, heat the remaining EVOO, and add onions, garlic, and sage. Sauté until onions are browned (about 7 minutes). Turn up the heat and add the roasted veggies.

Toss until veggies are hot and golden, and then add parsley. Season with salt and pepper to taste and enjoy!

Makes 2 servings.

VEGGIE EGG-WHITE FRITTATA

If you like basil, this turns a boring frittata into a lively dish. If you don't like basil, don't worry; I made it with asparagus, roasted peppers, and tomatoes this morning.

I had the veggies pre-chopped so when I got back from the gym, I put them in the frying pan with the EVOO. I sautéed for 2 to 3 minutes, then I poured the egg whites over and stuck the entire thing in the oven. You can add whatever vegetables you have in your fridge. It is healthy and simple to prepare.

You need to have a frying pan that is oven safe, completely melt proof, so you can put the entire thing in the oven. To not waste the egg yolk, it is best to buy egg whites in a carton. Twelve egg whites come out to roughly 2 ½ cups.

Ingredients:

1 Tablespoon EVOO
½ cup yellow onion, finely diced
4 garlic cloves, minced
12 pieces asparagus, chopped into 1-inch pieces
12 cherry tomatoes, halved
½ cup basil, julienned
12 egg whites, lightly beaten
Salt and pepper
Basil leaves, for garnish
4-8 teaspoons fresh salsa, for garnish (optional)

Directions:

Preheat oven to 350°F.

Heat oil in a 6-inch nonstick, oven-safe pan and sauté onions and garlic for 1 minute on medium-low heat. Add asparagus, sauté for 30 seconds, and then add tomatoes and basil. Season with sea salt and pepper.

Add egg whites to pan and mix briefly. Place in the oven for 8 - 10 minutes, or until done (eggs are solid and white). Garnish with 1 - 2 teaspoons of fresh salsa.

Makes 4-6 servings.

FALL BREAKFAST BOWL

This is a hearty breakfast for a cold, windy or snowy morning. This will fill your tummy with warm nutritious goodness so you are ready to face the day head-on. You can use tofu or black beans depending on what you have in the kitchen. I have used frozen chopped asparagus, mushrooms and broccoli, as substitutes. The key is to use brown rice cooked and left over from the night before.

Ingredients:

1 cup brown rice, cooked
1 cup frozen asparagus, chopped into 1-inch pieces
1 cup frozen peas and carrots
4 green onions (scallions), finely chopped
4 oz. extra firm tofu, chopped; or ½ cup black beans, drained and rinsed
½ cup roasted cashews or pecans, chopped
1 Tablespoon EVOO
Pinch sea salt
¼ teaspoon Braggs Amino Acid liquid

Directions:

In a saucepan add frozen vegetables, EVOO, and ½ the green onion; sauté about 7 minutes or until the vegetables are defrosted and browned. Mix in tofu/beans and brown rice; combine until heated, about 3 - 5 minutes. Stir in nuts and serve.

Makes 2 servings.

CHAPTER 4
Healthy Side Dishes

Side dishes such as bread, potatoes, dinner rolls, and pasta are often used as filler. These items are inflammatory and low in nutrients. They have no place at the table when healthier options can be made. Side dishes should enhance the nutrient content of the meal while providing diversified flavor.

It is my goal to present you with a variety of sides that make meal time more adventurous while providing lots of nutrients. All too often, people fall into the habit of preparing food the same way. This section provides you with variants on some old standbys that make for a big taste and nutritional difference.

SIMPLE BRUSSELS SPROUTS

As a child, I loathed these little green beauties — that's because they were boiled into oblivion. Over-boiling vegetables leaches the nutrients into the water and leaves the vegetables lifeless. At that point, it's probably better to drink the water!

Brussels sprouts are part of the cruciferous vegetable family. They are packed with cancer-fighting properties, which assist with the breakdown of toxins in our liver. Brussels sprouts have a whole new look when they are cooked this way, and they are a fall and winter favorite.

Ingredients:

1 pound fresh brussels sprouts; washed, trimmed, and cut in half

1 Tablespoon maple syrup

$1/3$ cup walnuts, toasted and chopped

1 teaspoon EVOO

$1/3$ cup chopped leeks (Use the white lower part of the bulb.)

Directions:

Bring a large pot of water to boil. Add brussels sprouts and blanch for 1 minute. Remove from boiling water, and move to a saucepan. Sauté on medium heat with EVOO and the leeks for 10 minutes, stirring rapidly.

In another small saucepan, toss the walnuts rapidly over medium heat until toasted (about 7 minutes). Be careful not to burn them. Remove brussels sprouts from heat, drizzle with maple syrup, and add toasted walnuts. Yum, yummm … good!

Makes 4 servings.

QUINOA SALAD

I'm always raving about quinoa; I absolutely love this super seed!

This salad, served cold, is a fantastic side dish to be paired with grilled vegetables, fish, or chicken or served alongside a leafy green salad. I have taken it to potlucks and it has always been a hit. Go ahead and try it, you will not be disappointed.

It is best to make the quinoa the day before so that it is cooled and can be combined with the other ingredients quickly. I prefer feta from sheep because the proteins are smaller and easier to digest; it causes less of a problem in folks with a dairy sensitivity.

Salad Ingredients:

1 cup quinoa
1 medium cucumber, peeled and diced
1/3 cup parsley, chopped
1 tomato, diced (I prefer an heirloom tomato or one fresh from the garden.)
1/2 cup sheep feta, crumbled
1/3 cup red onion, finely chopped
1/3 cup Kalamata olives, pitted and halved

Dressing Ingredients:

1/2 cup EVOO
1/4 cup red wine vinegar
1/4 teaspoon sea salt
1/2 teaspoon fresh or dried dill
2 Tablespoons fresh lemon juice

Directions:

To make the dressing, combine all dressing ingredients in a bowl and whisk.

To make the salad, add 2 cups water to a pot and bring to a boil. Add quinoa. Reduce heat to a simmer and set covered so that a bit of steam can escape from the pot. Quinoa is cooked when all water is absorbed and it can be fluffed with fork. Set quinoa aside to cool.

Prepare other vegetables and place in a bowl. Pour dressing over the chopped vegetables and mix thoroughly, allowing the vegetables to absorb the flavor of the dressing. Then, mix in the cooled quinoa.

Makes 6 servings.

QUINOA STUFFING

This is a nutritious, gluten-free alternative to traditional bread stuffing, and it is oh-so-much less inflammatory to your system. Remember, you need plant foods; only they provide the important phytonutrients and antioxidants that protect our cells from damage and keep our bodies from breaking down.

This dish is tasty and easy!

Ingredients:

1½ cup quinoa, rinsed and drained

1 cup green apple, chopped into quarter-inch pieces with skin

¼ cup dried cranberries

½ small brown onion, chopped

2 celery stalks, chopped into quarter-inch pieces

½ cup walnuts, chopped

⅓ cup roasted sunflower seeds

Directions:

Preheat oven to 350°F.

Toast the walnuts by adding them to a saucepan on medium heat and stirring them every 30 seconds for 5 minutes until brown. Be very careful; they can burn quickly.

Combine all ingredients in an oven-safe dish. Mix in the raw quinoa. Add 6 ounces of water to the dish and cover with a lid or aluminum foil. Bake for 40 minutes or until the quinoa is soft.

Makes 4 servings.

ROOT VEGETABLE MASH

Move aside, boring white potatoes! Here's something healthier—a combination of root vegetables in a delicious and nutritious mash. I only recommend peeling items that absolutely require it. The skin contains a lot of fiber, so it is better to leave it on.

Ingredients:

1 small purple turnip, washed and cubed

1 white potato, washed and cubed

1 sweet potato, washed and cubed

½ butternut squash (about 1 cup), peeled and cubed

2 Tablespoons EVOO

1 small brown or yellow onion, chopped

½ cup unsweetened rice, soy, or almond milk (your choice)

1 teaspoon sea salt

Salt and black pepper to taste

Directions:

Add the turnip, potatoes, and squash to a large soup pot. Cover with water and boil until a knife can easily go through the vegetables. Drain water and let the veggies sit in the pot.

In a frying pan, add EVOO and the chopped onion. Sauté on medium heat until onions turn translucent. Mash all cooked veggies in soup pot with a potato masher. Add the cooked onions, your choice of milk, and salt and pepper. Whip all ingredients together. More milk can be added to enhance the creaminess.

Makes 4 servings.

CUBAN-STYLE BLACK BEANS

The key to flavor in this recipe is to cover the beans so that they absorb the flavors of the herbs. This turns boring black beans into a tasty side dish filled with fiber and protein.

Ingredients:

2 teaspoons EVOO
½ cup brown onion, chopped
1 Tablespoon Braggs® Amino Acids Liquid Seasoning
1 teaspoon cumin, ground
2 garlic cloves, crushed
2 cups cooked black beans
½ cup cilantro, chopped
1 lime, juiced
Salt and black pepper to taste
Hot sauce to taste

Directions:

Heat oil in a saucepan and add garlic and onions. Sauté for 5 minutes, stirring regularly. Add beans, Braggs®, cilantro, cumin, lime, and pepper. Cover and reduce heat to low. Cook for 10 minutes. Add salt and pepper to taste and serve with hot sauce on the side.

Makes 2 servings.

SWEET POTATO FRIES

You may even be able to win the kids over with this one! Sweet potatoes (and all orange colored vegetables) are high in vitamin A, which is great for our immune system and is an antioxidant to our eye tissue. Sweet potatoes are naturally sweet and delicious, from nature's farm to your mouth.

Ingredients:

2 medium sweet potatoes, washed and sliced lengthwise into half-inch thick strips
1 Tablespoon EVOO
½ teaspoon sea salt
½ teaspoon dried thyme
¼ teaspoon chili powder
¼ teaspoon garlic powder

Directions:

Preheat oven to 350°F.

Place the sweet potatoes on a baking tray with edges. In a small bowl, mix the EVOO, seasonings, and herbs. Drizzle EVOO mixture over sweet potatoes and toss by hand to coat all sides.

Place in oven to bake. Adjust every 15 minutes by shaking the pan so that the fries do not stick to the baking sheet. Fries are done when slightly brown on at least 2 sides and a fork can be easily inserted.

Makes 4 servings.

WILD RICE STUFFING

This is another gluten-free stuffing idea for health conscious families everywhere! This is not just a stuffing; it is an amazing side dish for almost everything, especially fish or poultry. It is a delight for vegetarians, and it is packed with nutrients all by itself.

Cooked wild rice has a rich, nutty flavor—sometimes described as a smoky flavor—and a texture that is delightfully chewy. Wild rice is actually a grass, and it towers over other grains when it comes to amounts of protein, minerals, B vitamins, and folic acid. While the protein content of a half cup of cooked wild rice measures 3.3 grams, that same quantity of long grain brown rice contains only 2 grams.

Ingredients:

2 cups wild rice
4 cups vegetable or chicken broth
½ cup pine nuts
¾ cup dried cranberries
2 Tablespoons EVOO
2 stalks celery, finely chopped
2 carrots, finely chopped
1 medium brown onion, finely chopped
1 Tablespoon fresh thyme leaves
1 Tablespoon fresh sage, chopped
½ cup parsley, chopped
Sea salt and fresh ground pepper to taste

Directions:

Preheat oven to 350°F.

Simmer rice in broth for 40 minutes, or until rice is tender. It will still be runny with liquid in the bottom.

Toast pine nuts in a skillet on stove, turning frequently so that they don't burn. After 3 to 5 minutes, transfer to a bowl.

Add 1 Tablespoon of EVOO to a skillet over medium heat. Swirl and add carrots, celery, and onion. Sauté for about 5 minutes, then add thyme, sage, and parsley. Sauté for 1 minute more.

In a large mixing bowl, add the rice, vegetable and herb mixture, toasted pine nuts, cranberries, and fresh ground pepper and sea salt to taste.

With the remaining Tablespoon of EVOO, coat a casserole dish and add the mixture. Cover and bake for 20 minutes.

Makes 6 servings.

CURRIED QUINOA WITH PECANS

The first time I made this I didn't have any lentils, so I used wild rice and it still turned out fantastic. The lentils add a bit more depth to it as a satisfying healthy carbohydrate meal addition. The dates and nuts add just the right amount of crunch and sweetness. Mmmm good…

Ingredients:

2 cups water
2 Tablespoons EVOO
1 onion, finely chopped (about 1 cup)
¾ cup quinoa, rinsed and drained
2 teaspoons curry powder or curry seasoning powder
½ cup cooked lentils
½ cup pitted prunes or dates, finely chopped
¼ cup roasted pecans, chopped
Pinch sea salt

Directions:

In a medium saucepan, bring lentils, sea salt and water to a boil. Add quinoa to water mixture, and reduce to a simmer. Quinoa/lentils are done when all water evaporates and can be fluffed with a fork; about 20 minutes. Set aside covered.

In a skillet over medium heat, toast pecans, stirring frequently for 5 to 7 minutes.

Heat EVOO in medium skillet. Add onion and curry seasoning, sauté for 3 to 4 minutes or until translucent. Stir in cooked quinoa and lentils, heat for 5 minutes. Then mix in prunes and pecans, and serve.

Makes 4 servings.

CHAPTER 5
Healthy Salads

Salads don't have to just come in leafy greens. They can be protein packed, filled with fiber, and a refreshing addition to any meal! I keep a big bowl of salad in my fridge at all times. When I come home starving, I make a salad, and it helps hold me over until I can cook the main course.

Using salad as filler is a healthier alternative than relying on high-calorie, empty-nutrient snack foods. Salads provide nutrients, antioxidants, and protective components that help us detoxify. Salads should include dark leafy greens and a rainbow of colors from other vegetables. This is the winning combination of fiber, vitamins, minerals, and phytochemicals that nature provides for us to generate energy and rebuild a healthy cellular matrix.

Dressings are equally important. Many people have a nice salad and completely blow it with the dressing. Salad dressing should be as fresh as the salad that it is drizzled on! Dressing should have natural ingredients that complement the salad. A good dressing will help bring out the flavor of the salad itself. I have a few dressings in this section to help you explore making salad dressing at home. Once you do it, you will realize how easy it is and, more importantly, how much better it tastes!

Making your own salad dressing is so simple and it is what I recommend. However, purchasing pre-made salad dressing is an option if you choose your brands wisely. Often, pre-made dressings have preservatives, cheap oils, and chemicals that are not healthy at all. If you want to purchase a salad dressing, I recommend vinaigrette, such as Newman's Own or Annie's Organics. If you're feeling adventurous, go ahead and try the dressing recipes in this section; you just might be pleasantly surprised!

BASIC LIME AND HONEY DRESSING

This one can sit for at least two days in the fridge before the basil starts to get a tad bit brown. The lime juice, when combined with the honey, gives it a bit of sweet and sour flavor that avoids the bite of using vinegar.

Ingredients:

2 Tablespoons EVOO
1 lime, juiced
1 Tablespoon honey
2 pinches of sea salt
5 large basil leaves

Directions:

Blend in a food processor or blender. Be careful to stir from the bottom as honey has a tendency to settle to the bottom. Drizzle over salad.

VERSATILE VINAIGRETTE

Here's a delightful dressing recipe that will last in your fridge for up to a month!

Ingredients:

½ cup fresh lemon juice
2/3 cup EVOO
3 garlic cloves, crushed or minced
1½ teaspoons spicy brown mustard
1 teaspoon minced fresh thyme or ¼ teaspoon dried thyme
1 Tablespoon minced fresh tarragon, basil, or dill (Use 1 teaspoon if herbs are dried.)
½ teaspoon sea salt
½ teaspoon coarsely ground black pepper

Directions:

Place all ingredients in a jar with a tight-fitting lid and shake vigorously to blend.

Serve immediately or refrigerate for later.

Shake before using.

ARUGULA WITH BLUE CHEESE

The Brits call it rocket and the Italians call it arugula. Whatever you name it, everyone at the dinner table will call it delicious!

Arugula is super flavorful and a bit bitter. My recommendation is to buy the baby arugula — the leaves are more tender and soak up the dressing well and it is also less bitter than the adult leaves.

You can use any cheese with this salad or none at all. A small amount of blue cheese goes a long way. The blue cheese has a strong flavor that pairs well with the flavor of the arugula and the sweetness of the pears — a true flavor explosion!

Salad Ingredients:

1 bag (about 10 to 12 ounces) of pre-washed baby arugula
1/3 cup crumbled blue cheese
1/3 cup pine nuts
1/3 cup raw pecans, chopped
1 pear; peeled, cored and thinly sliced
1 lemon, juiced

Dressing Ingredients:

1 Tablespoon EVOO
2 teaspoons fresh lemon juice
1/3 teaspoon sea salt

Dressing Directions:

To prepare the dressing, simply whisk the dressing ingredients together.

Salad Directions:

Take pre-washed arugula, pat dry and place in a bowl. In a saucepan, toast the pine nuts and pecans on medium heat. Stir regularly so as to not to burn (about 5 to 7 minutes). Remove from heat and set aside.

Peel and core the pear, slicing it into eighths. Squeeze lemon over the pear to prevent it from browning.

Toss blue cheese, pine nuts, pecans, and arugula in a bowl. Drizzle on dressing and mix thoroughly. Lay pears on top to display or set out on individual plates.

Makes 2 servings.

BLACK BEAN SALAD

Often, when people think of salads, they think of leafy greens. This salad is cool, refreshing, and gives you your daily dose of fruits, vegetables, and fiber.

I once took this to a party on top of a bed of leafy greens instead of tossing it into the salad. The partygoers ate just the mix of black beans off the top of the bed of lettuce, never bothered with the greens underneath, and said it was the best salad they ever had. If you don't make it too spicy this will be a winner with kids as well.

Ingredients:

1 (15 oz.) can of black beans, rinsed and drained
1 mango, diced (The ideal mango is ripe and juicy.)
½ red bell pepper, diced small
1 scallion, thinly sliced
2 Tablespoons EVOO
2 teaspoons red wine vinegar or fresh lime juice
1 teaspoon jalapeno, minced
1 Tablespoon fresh cilantro, chopped
1 pinch sea salt
2 Tablespoons crumbled goat cheese

Directions:

Mix everything but the cheese together in a bowl. Allow it to marinate in the refrigerator for 1 hour. Sprinkle with goat cheese just before serving.

Makes 2 servings.

CABBAGE WITH CARROT AND GINGER DRESSING

Cabbage is a member of the cruciferous vegetable family, and it helps us detoxify from harmful cancer-causing substances. This is a nice alternative to a traditional lettuce based salad. And it will keep in the fridge for two days. The cabbage is crunchy and refreshing, and the dressing is full of flavor. You will not be disappointed.

Dressing Ingredients:

½ cup carrots, grated
2 Tablespoons fresh ginger, grated
2 Tablespoons rice vinegar
1 Tablespoon toasted sesame oil
2 teaspoons grape seed oil
1 teaspoon maple syrup or honey or 5 drops liquid stevia, unflavored

To prepare dressing, simply whisk or blend all ingredients in food processor until smooth.

Salad Ingredients:

4 cups cabbage (approximately ½ head), thinly sliced
1 medium size radicchio head, thinly sliced
½ cup red or sweet onion, thinly sliced
2 Tablespoons toasted sesame seeds
1 avocado, thinly sliced

Salad Directions:

Combine in a bowl, drizzle dressing on top, and serve.

Note: When I first made this, I didn't use radicchio or sesame seeds, and it still came out amazing! The dressing is superb!

Makes 2 servings.

COLORFUL ROMAINE BLEND

This is a rainbow of colors. The beets and artichokes are excellent for liver purification. The black beans provide protein and fiber. Carrots are high in vitamin A, and the olives add a kick of flavor.

All ingredients can be tossed together ahead of time, except the beets. Beets mixed into a salad will turn it a strange pink color. Place the grated beets to the side of the bowl or plate. They can be mixed in after it is served.

Dressing Ingredients:

2 Tablespoons EVOO
1 lime, juiced
1 Tablespoon honey
2 pinches of sea salt
5 large basil leaves

Salad Ingredients:

4 to 6 large romaine leaves, washed and chopped
1 small to medium beet, washed and grated raw
1 large carrot, washed and grated raw
4 artichoke hearts in water, drained and sliced into quarters
10 pitted Kalamata olives, sliced in halves
1 (15 oz.) can black beans, rinsed and drained

Directions:

In a bowl, mix all ingredients together except for the beets. Place the beets in one corner of the bowl or in a separate storage container.

When ready to serve, drizzle the dressing on top, and enjoy!

Makes 2 servings.

SOUTHERN-STYLE SLAW

This is a variant of creamy coleslaw. The mustard and cayenne give it another dimension of flavor. This is great paired with baked beans, chicken or fish. This is an enjoyable way to consume one to two cups of cabbage in a cool, creamy, and crisp way.

Naturally packed with antioxidants and high in vitamin C, cabbage has been ranked at the top of the list of foods that aid cancer prevention. Don't forget the parsley! It also helps to neutralize cancer-causing compounds.

Ingredients:

4 cups green or red cabbage, thinly sliced
2 medium carrots, grated
1 medium red bell pepper (about 1 cup), thinly sliced
3 Tablespoons mayonnaise
¼ cup almond milk, unsweetened
2 Tablespoons whole grain mustard without sugar
1 Tablespoon apple cider vinegar
3 drops liquid stevia, vanilla flavor
½ teaspoon sea salt
1 pinch of cayenne pepper
½ cup parsley, chopped

Directions:

In a bowl, whisk together mayonnaise, almond milk, mustard, apple cider vinegar, stevia, salt, and cayenne pepper. In a separate bowl, combine cabbage, carrots, and bell pepper. Pour liquid mixture over cabbage mixture and toss. Chill and sprinkle with parsley before serving.

Makes 4 servings.

THREE BEAN TWISTER

This salad tastes even better the next day after the dressing has been left to marinate over the beans. I prefer using the thinner green beans. They are often called haricot vert, which simply means "green bean" in French. They are less stringy and have a nice flavor — just be careful to not overcook them.

Green beans are high in minerals, vitamin C, and manganese, and they help with cardiovascular health. Chickpeas are high in fiber, molybdenum, manganese, and folic acid. The edamame complete this salad with a hefty dose of protein, calcium, and vitamin A. Go on; give it a twist! Your body will thank you.

Ingredients:

Zest of 2 lemons (approximately 2 Tablespoons)
¼ cup grape seed oil
¼ cup fresh lemon juice
½ teaspoon sea salt
2 drops liquid stevia, lemon flavor
1 (10 oz.) bag frozen, shelled edamame
1 can chickpeas, rinsed and drained
10 ounces fresh green beans, cut into
1-inch pieces
6 scallions, thinly chopped

Directions:

Zest the lemon using a small hand grater or a special kitchen tool called a microplane.

In a serving bowl, whisk together lemon zest, oil, lemon juice, salt, and stevia. Set aside.

Place 1 inch of water in a pot and bring to a boil. Place edamame in a steamer in the pot and steam for 3 minutes to defrost and quickly steam. Add chickpeas and steam for 4 additional minutes. Pour into a bowl and pat dry. Add to liquid mixture.

In the same saucepan, bring another inch of water to boil, steam green beans until bright green but still crunchy (about 4 to 5 minutes). Remove from pot and rinse under cold water. Drain and pat dry.

Add green beans and scallions to chickpea mixture, toss, and add sea salt to taste.

Makes 4 servings.

TUSCAN BEAN & VEGETABLE SALAD

This can be paired so nicely with the wild rice stuffing! You can really taste the celery and red onion combined with the white beans here. The dressing gives a tangy sweet and sour lemon twist, which is perfect with fish. Cannellini beans have a lot to offer, including fiber, calcium, folic acid, and as much iron as beef! Go ahead, dig in!

Ingredients:

2 (15 oz.) cans cannellini beans (also called white beans), drained and rinsed
1 stalk celery, diced
¼ cup Kalamata olives, chopped
1 Tablespoon fresh basil, chopped
2 Tablespoons parsley, chopped
1 head romaine lettuce, chopped
1 small red onion, finely chopped
1 pinch of sea salt
6 Tablespoons EVOO
¼ cup fresh lemon juice
2 to 4 drops liquid, lemon flavor

Directions:

For the dressing, whisk together the EVOO and lemon juice with the stevia and add the salt. In a separate bowl, mix all remaining salad ingredients together and add dressing as desired.

Makes 4 servings.

AVOCADO ZUCCHINI SALAD

Ahhh the amazing avocado, the little darling of the west coast. Avocados provide us with unique health benefits precisely because of its unusual fat composition.

The fats in avocados help us digest special fat-soluble antioxidants called carotenoids as well as other fat-soluble vitamins. These antioxidants and vitamins are important for optimal health. We often don't think of eating zucchini raw but it's just great, I often add raw shredded zucchini to salads.

Ingredients:

2 avocados, diced
1 zucchini, diced
2 Tablespoons lemon juice
2 Tablespoons basil, finely chopped
1 Tablespoon EVOO
1 Tablespoon chives, minced
5 drops liquid stevia, plain
2 teaspoons sea salt

Directions:

In a measuring cup whisk the lemon juice, EVOO, stevia, and sea salt.
Mix avocados, zucchini, and basil until combined, drizzle with dressing and sprinkle with chopped chives.

Makes 4 servings.

SALAD DRESSINGS

Salad dressings are not just for salads, they can be used as vegetable marinades, or to zip up the flavor of rice or quinoa. Here are a few salad dressings for you to try out:

CHAMPAGNE VINAIGRETTE

2 Tablespoons champagne vinegar

1 Tablespoon fresh parsley, chopped

1 Tablespoon shallots, chopped

⅓ cup EVOO

Pinch of sea salt and pepper

Whisk together

RED WINE VINAIGRETTE

1 Tablespoon red wine vinegar

1 teaspoon mustard

1 garlic clove, minced

⅓ cup EVOO

Pinch of sea salt and pepper

Whisk together

APPLE CIDER VINAIGRETTE

2 Tablespoons apple cider vinegar

1 Tablespoon mustard

4 drops vanilla flavored stevia

¼ cup EVOO

Pinch of sea salt and pepper

Whisk together

LIME MINT DRESSING

1 Tablespoon lime juice

3 Tablespoons mint, chopped

¼ cup EVOO

Pinch of sea salt and pepper

Whisk together

CILANTRO SESAME DRESSING

2 Tablespoons sesame oil

½ teaspoon fresh ginger, grated

½ teaspoon jalapeno, minced

2 teaspoons cilantro, chopped

Pinch of sea salt and pepper

Whisk together

CHAPTER 6
Healthy Soups

I know that your time is valuable, so I have designed soup recipes that can be prepared as a complement to any meal, or served alone as a main course.

Soups are also a great way to consume a lot of vegetables, and be deeply warmed and nourished. When pureed, kids will gobble them up and ask for seconds. During the colder months, soup can be eaten when salads lose their appeal. They are easier to digest and very satisfying.

The fall and winter season also lend themselves to the making of nutrient-dense hearty soups and stews. This is a great time of year to experiment and get your vegetables! Making your own soup can be easy, and as it becomes more second nature over time, you can add handfuls of rice, lentils, or whatever vegetables you have in your kitchen.

For a heartier option, soups can be ladled over wild rice, quinoa, spinach, or corn. They can be made in large pots ahead of time and frozen for future use. I encourage you to make up a big batch on a Sunday and enjoy it for a few hearty meals throughout the week.

VEGETABLE MINESTRONE

This is an old favorite and a great way to get your vegetables! Once the vegetables are chopped, the soup cooks quickly, so put your kids to work and get them to prep the vegetables for you. Chopping vegetables is a great way to introduce children to cooking and get them excited about food.

Ingredients:

1 Tablespoon EVOO
1 pound leeks white bulbs, chopped or white bulbs of leeks
2 large carrots, diced in half-inch pieces
8 cups organic, low sodium vegetable broth
½ cup wild rice
1 (15 oz.) can cannellini beans, drained and rinsed
1 cup string beans, chopped into half-inch pieces
1 cup zucchini, diced
1 cup frozen green peas
1 cup asparagus, chopped into half-inch pieces
1 Tablespoon parsley, chopped
1 Tablespoon basil, chopped
2 scallions, thinly sliced
1 garlic clove, finely chopped
2 Tablespoons parmesan cheese (optional)

Directions:

In a large soup pot, add the oil, leeks, and carrots with 1 Tablespoon of water. Cover and cook for 15 minutes. Add 6 cups of broth, bring to boil, and add wild rice. Cook for 10 to 15 minutes. Add cannellini beans, string beans, zucchini, peas, and asparagus, and simmer on medium heat for 10 minutes.

In a small bowl, mix parsley, basil, scallions, and garlic. Stir into soup. Add remaining broth if the soup is too thick. The soup is done when the rice is cooked. Sprinkle parmesan before serving (optional).

Makes 6 servings.

NO CREAM OF ASPARAGUS

The rice blends here to create a pseudo-cream, dairy-free base. This recipe can also be made with broccoli; just reserve about half a cup of the chopped florets to be used at the end where you stir in the asparagus tips. I prefer the thinner asparagus because it is more tender. Asparagus is high in potassium, folic acid, and vitamin C, and it helps build healthy digestive bacteria.

Ingredients:

2 pounds asparagus

2 Tablespoons EVOO

2 medium brown onions (about 3 cups), chopped

1/3 cup uncooked brown basmati rice

8 cups organic, low sodium vegetable broth

2 sprigs thyme

Sea salt and pepper to taste

Directions:

Wash the asparagus, and trim 1 inch off the bottom of each. Then chop into half-inch pieces, and set the top part of the asparagus aside, these are known as the asparagus tips.

Add the oil and onions to a soup pot and sauté on medium heat for about 5 minutes. Stir in asparagus pieces, rice, thyme, and vegetable broth. Reduce heat and cook covered for about 35 minutes or until rice is cooked. Remove thyme with a slotted spoon.

Ladle soup into blender and puree. You won't be able to fit all the soup in the blender at once, so do it in 2 to 3 batches. Return blended soup to pot and add asparagus tips. Simmer 2 to 3 minutes and serve.

Makes 6 servings.

LENTIL SOUP

There are many types of lentils: brown, red, French green, and regular. I prefer French green, and health food stores typically carry these lentils in the bulk section. They are smaller than other lentil varieties and maintain their shape.

Lentils help to lower cholesterol and blood sugar with their fiber content. They are high in six minerals, and they are an excellent source of folic acid.

If too much of the water evaporates, you will get lentil stew instead of soup. I like to use salt, it livens up the lentils. I then season to just under the desired taste and then finish with Braggs® Amino Acids when serving. It adds a nice touch. Remember, you can always add more sea salt if there isn't enough flavor.

Ingredients:

4 medium onions (about 4 cups), diced

1 Tablespoon EVOO

1 Tablespoon sea salt

½ cup cilantro, chopped

2 to 4 teaspoons garlic, chopped

1 Tablespoon paprika

1 pound lentils

6 cups water

Directions:

In a large pot, add onions, garlic, and oil. Cook on medium heat, stirring occasionally. Be careful to not let the onions stick and burn. Cook until the onions are translucent. (This is also called sweating the onions.)

Wash the lentils and add to the onions and garlic.

Add water to the pot, bring to a boil, and add cilantro. Lower heat and simmer approximately 1½ to 2 hours.

Season with sea salt and/or Braggs® Amino Acids to taste.

Makes 6 servings.

HOMEMADE VEGETABLE SOUP

This is a basic soup recipe that can be modified into chicken soup.

Ingredients:

8 cups organic, low sodium vegetable broth
2 carrots, chopped or sliced
2 stalks celery, chopped
½ onion or 4 scallions, chopped
2 leaves swiss chard or bok choy, chopped
2 garlic cloves, crushed or thinly sliced
1 teaspoon sea salt

Directions:

Bring broth to a boil. Add carrots, onion, celery, and garlic, cover, and simmer for 1½ hours.

Twenty minutes before the soup is finished, taste and add seasoning as desired. Add 2 leaves of chopped swiss chard or bok choy. Stir and replace lid.

Serve and enjoy.

NOTE: This soup can be modified to homemade chicken soup by adding chicken broth and a whole, organic chicken. Read on ...

Makes 6 servings.

CHICKEN SOUP VARIATION

Ingredients:

Whole, organic chicken
4 cups organic chicken broth
Sea salt and pepper to taste
1 orange, juiced

Directions:

Preheat oven to 400°F.

Place the washed and rinsed chicken in an ovenproof soup pot. Add chicken broth and 4 cups of water, salt and pepper, and the orange juice. Cook covered in the oven for 1 hour.

Remove from oven. Remove chicken from pot and remove the skin. Chop up breast meat and leg meat and add back to the pot. Add vegetables and cook 40 minutes. Add the greens and cook for 20 minutes. Season to taste and enjoy!

Makes 6 servings.

HALIBUT AND CHICKPEA SOUP

This soup is delicious. The white wine sautéed with the herbs and fennel adds a nice flavor. The fish is a great protein complement, and it is tender and juicy.

Ingredients:

2 teaspoons EVOO
1 small white potato, washed and chopped into half-inch cubes
¼ cup parsley, finely chopped
¾ cup onion, finely chopped
¼ cup fennel bulb, thinly sliced
1 fresh rosemary sprig (approximately 4 inches long)
4 tomatoes, roughly chopped
1 (15 oz.) can chickpeas, drained and rinsed
½ cup dry white wine
6 cups organic, low sodium chicken broth
1 pound white fish fillets (halibut, turbot, or Pacific cod)
Sea salt and pepper to taste

Directions:

Heat 1 teaspoon of EVOO in a saucepan on medium heat. Add onion and cook for 3 minutes. Add fennel, rosemary, tomatoes, chickpeas, potato, wine, and broth. Cover and bring to boil for 20 minutes or until the potato is soft.

Cut fish into 1-inch chunks and add to boiling broth. Reduce heat and simmer until fish is cooked through or flakes when pulled apart with a fork (about 3 minutes). Remove rosemary sprig with a slotted spoon and add salt and pepper to taste. Just before serving, sprinkle with chopped, fresh parsley and the remaining teaspoon of EVOO.

Makes 6 servings.

CAULIFLOWER, FENNEL, AND LEEK SOUP

Leeks are less strong in flavor than onions, and the fennel adds a lovely taste. Blended cauliflower gives a creamy consistency. This soup is filled with health promoting properties that assist with detoxification and enhance immune system function.

Ingredients:

1 Tablespoon coconut oil (The virgin coconut oil has a coconut taste, and the regular does not—
    just a matter of preference.)
1 large leek, thinly sliced
2 stalks celery, finely chopped
1 fennel bulb, thinly chopped
1 head cauliflower, cored and chopped
3 cups organic, low sodium vegetable broth
1 cup unsweetened almond milk
2 Tablespoons almond oil
¼ cup fresh basil leaves for garnish

Directions:

In a soup pot, sauté coconut oil, leek, celery, and fennel for about 5 minutes. Add cauliflower and broth and cook 20 minutes covered. Stir in almond milk and remove from heat.

Ladle soup from the soup pot into a food processor or blender. Blend until smooth. (You may need to do this in 3 to 4 batches as it won't all fit at once.) Once blended, pour the soup from the blender back into the soup pot. Stir in 1 Tablespoon of almond oil.

Before serving, drizzle with remaining almond oil and garnish with fresh basil leaves.

Makes 6 servings.

BROCCOLI-CAULIFLOWER SOUP

This healthful soup combines two cancer-fighting vegetables for a smooth, creamy soup. Remember, soups can be frozen and eaten at another time.

Ingredients:

2 heads of broccoli, cut into florets

1 small head of cauliflower, cut into florets

1 cup green onions and tops, chopped

2 teaspoons EVOO

3 cups organic chicken broth, low sodium

1⅓ cups parsnips, peeled and chopped

3 Tablespoons chives, finely chopped

2½ teaspoons dried basil

1½ cups unsweetened almond milk

Sea salt and pepper to taste

Directions:

In a deep, large saucepan sauté green onions in EVOO until tender (about 4 minutes).

Stir in chicken broth, chopped vegetables, and spices. Reduce heat and simmer uncovered until parsnips are tender (15 to 20 minutes).

Process in a food processor or with a blender wand until smooth. Add milk and simmer another 5 minutes. Season to taste.

Makes 6 servings.

TORTILLA AVOCADO SOUP

This soup is easy, and delicious. Just get the tortillas toasting, then chop up the avocado and cilantro and set aside. Puréeing some of the soup creates a creamy texture without any cream. Note that corn is a genetically modified crop; it is best to buy organic corn whenever possible.

Ingredients:

3 6-inch organic corn tortillas
2 Tablespoons EVOO, divided
½ teaspoon cumin
1 small yellow onion, chopped
3 cups organic corn kernels, fresh or frozen and thawed
2 ½ cups low-sodium vegetable broth
1 small red bell pepper, cored, seeded, and diced
1 small avocado, diced
¼ cup fresh cilantro, chopped

Directions:

Preheat oven to 375°F.

Stack tortillas and cut into ¼-inch strips. In a medium bowl, toss together with 1 tablespoon EVOO and cumin. Spread in a single layer on a large baking sheet and sprinkle with salt. Bake, turning frequently, until golden brown, 10-15 minutes. Remove from oven and let cool slightly.

While tortillas are cooking, in a medium pot, heat remaining 1 tablespoon EVOO and cook onion on medium-high for 3 minutes. Add corn, bell pepper, and 2 cups broth. Bring to a boil, reduce heat, and cook for 2-3 minutes, until corn is tender. Using a food processor or blender, purée about half of the soup, in batches, until smooth. Then add it back to the other half of soup.

To serve, divide avocado, cilantro, and tortilla strips between four serving bowls, layering on bottom. Ladle soup over ingredients; serve hot.

Makes 4 servings.

CHAPTER 7
Healthy Vegetarian Recipes

Choosing to be a vegetarian requires an additional commitment to food preparation. Often, a busy life on the go does not lend itself to healthy vegetarianism. All too often, busy vegetarians find themselves eating unhealthy snack foods and fast foods due to the inability to prepare healthy vegetarian meals.

Remember, that the word vegetable is in the word vegetarian, and when you embark on the commitment to vegetarianism, you must also commit to buying and preparing vegetables. These recipes are delicious, nutritious, and can be made to eat over the course of a few days. Enjoy!

ROASTED PEPPER AND BLACK BEAN TACOS

Roasted peppers add a totally different flavor to a bean taco. This can be made low-carb by placing this mixture in swiss chard or a lettuce leaf, adding toppings, and rolling it. This recipe is great when taken for lunch the next day. You can roll the tacos and place in a glass container or simply combine all the fillings and toppings with chopped lettuce for a taco salad.

Roasted Peppers & Onions Ingredients:

3 red bell peppers (about 3 cups), thinly sliced
1 large onion (about 1½ cups), thinly sliced
1 Tablespoon EVOO

Taco Ingredients:

2 Tablespoons EVOO
1 medium onion (about 1 cup), chopped
6 garlic cloves (about 2 Tablespoons), minced
2 (15 oz.) cans black beans, drained and rinsed
1 (15 oz.) can diced, organic, fire-roasted tomatoes
1 Tablespoon chili powder
1 Tablespoon ground cumin
Hot sauce to taste
16 organic corn taco shells, warmed

Toppings Ingredients:

3 cups romaine lettuce, shredded
1 (16 oz.) container salsa, fresh or jarred
2 large tomatoes (about 2 cups), diced
2 avocados (about 2 cups), diced

Directions:

Preheat oven to 450°F.

Roasted Peppers and Onions:

Toss peppers and onions with oil on a large baking sheet. Season with salt and pepper. Roast 15 minutes, stir, and roast 15 minutes more or until vegetables are tender and peppers are beginning to blacken. Transfer to a small bowl.

Tacos:

Heat oil in a large pot over medium heat. Add onion and garlic, and sauté 5 to 7 minutes or until soft. Stir in beans, tomatoes, chili powder, cumin, hot sauce, and 1 cup water. Season with sea salt and pepper. Reduce heat to medium-low and simmer 15 minutes or until most of the liquid has evaporated, stirring occasionally. Add seasonings to taste. Transfer to a serving bowl.

Makes 6 servings.

THREE AMIGOS CASSEROLE

Three amigos refer to the practice of growing beans, corn, and squash together. This filling casserole can be frozen for an upcoming party or freshly made for dinner. This is a mild-tasting dish and the polenta makes it a bit sweet and very filling. The hardest preparation in this recipe comes from peeling and cutting the kabocha squash; ask a man for help with this part of the recipe.

Polenta Topping Ingredients:

1½ cups yellow cornmeal
1 Tablespoon chili powder
¾ teaspoon sea salt

Note: Polenta can be purchased pre-mixed and mashed for this dish; just add chili powder.

Filling Ingredients:

3 Tablespoons EVOO, divided
1 small onion (about 1 cup), chopped
1 large red or yellow bell pepper (about 1 cup), diced into 1-inch cubes
1 pound (about 2 cups) kabocha squash, peeled and cut into 1-inch cubes
1 (15 oz.) can diced tomatoes
2 cloves (about 2 teaspoons) garlic, minced
1 teaspoon ground cumin
1 teaspoon ground coriander
½ teaspoon sea salt
1 (15 oz.) can black beans, drained and rinsed
1 cup frozen corn kernels, thawed

Polenta Topping Directions:

Whisk together cornmeal, chili powder, salt, and 4½ cups water in a double boiler or in a large metal bowl over barely simmering water. Cook 40 minutes or until polenta is thick and stiff, stirring 3 or 4 times. Remove from heat.

Filling Directions:

Preheat oven to 375°F.

Heat 2 Tablespoons of EVOO in a large saucepan over medium heat. Add onion and cook 7 minutes or until softened, stirring often. Add bell pepper and cook 5 minutes more, stirring often.

Stir in squash, tomatoes, garlic, coriander, and cumin. Cook 5 minutes, stirring occasionally. Stir in half a cup of water and salt. Bring mixture to a boil. Reduce heat to medium-low and simmer partially covered for 20 minutes or until squash is tender. Stir in beans and corn and cook 5 minutes or until slightly thickened, stirring occasionally.

Coat an 8 × 11 baking dish with cooking spray. Spread 2 cups of polenta over the bottom of prepared dish. Spoon squash mixture over polenta. Smooth remaining polenta (about 2½ cups) over the top. Score casserole into 6 squares with a knife. Brush top with remaining Tablespoon of oil. Bake 30 minutes or until heated through and top is lightly browned.

Makes 6 servings.

SQUASH AND BLACK BEAN ENCHILADAS

This is a tasty version of a classic dish, which can be totally dairy-free if you like. Take it to a potluck or feed the whole family; it will raise conversation wherever you go. The beans and rice provide fiber and protein, the butternut squash provides vitamin A and folic acid, the cilantro is filled with phytonutrients, and the remaining ingredients all contribute their share to make this a family favorite.

Ingredients:

2 cups cooked brown rice
2 cups black beans, drained and rinsed
1½ cups butternut squash, peeled and cubed
1 small onion, diced
1 bell pepper, cored and diced
1 cup fresh or frozen corn kernels
1 (4 oz.) can diced green chilies, drained
10 sprigs cilantro, chopped
6 ounces sharp cheddar cheese or dairy-free alternative, grated and divided
Sea salt to taste
1 (15 oz.) can red enchilada sauce, gluten-free
1 dozen corn tortillas, fresh if possible
1 (15 oz.) can green enchilada sauce, gluten-free

Directions:

Preheat oven to 350°F.

In a sauce pot, steam butternut squash until a knife slices through easily. Remove from heat and mash.

Combine rice, beans, squash, onion, pepper, corn, chilies, cilantro, and 4 ounces of cheese in a large mixing bowl. Use a potato masher to thoroughly combine these ingredients. Season with sea salt and mix well.

Pour red enchilada sauce into a deep plate; dip each tortilla to coat. Fill each tortilla with one large spoonful of enchilada mixture, roll tightly, and place in a 9 × 13 baking dish or lasagna dish. When dish is full, cover enchiladas with green enchilada sauce.

Cover with foil and bake 45 minutes. Remove foil and top enchiladas with remaining cheese. Bake 10 more minutes.

Makes 6 servings.

SPAGHETTI SQUASH PRIMAVERA

Are you in the mood for pasta, but not the bloating, inflammation, or carbohydrates? Get ready for the spaghetti vegetable alternative. Be sure to cook the squash first while you prepare the rest of the vegetables. Spaghetti squash is high in vitamin C, B vitamins, and potassium. It shreds beautifully.

Ingredients:

1 medium spaghetti squash
1½ carrots, diagonally sliced
½ cup celery, diced
3 cloves garlic, crushed
1½ cups cabbage, shredded
1 small zucchini, chopped
1 (16 oz.) can pinto or white cannellini beans, drained and rinsed
1 large tomato, chopped
1/3 cup apple juice
1 teaspoon dried thyme
1 teaspoon dried parsley
½ teaspoon garlic powder
1 cup marinara sauce
1 head romaine lettuce
2 Tablespoons Parmesan cheese (optional)

Directions:

Preheat oven to 350°F.

Slice spaghetti squash in half lengthwise. Remove seeds with a spoon. Place both halves cut-side down on a baking sheet and bake for 45 minutes.

In a large pot, sauté carrots and celery in 2 Tablespoons of water for 10 minutes. Add garlic, cabbage, and zucchini, and cook covered for another 10 minutes. Stir in all remaining ingredients except for Marinara sauce. Cover and simmer for about 10 minutes or until carrots are tender.

Remove squash from oven and let cool for about 15 minutes. Using a fork with one hand, and holding the squash with the other, scrape the flesh of the squash into spaghetti-like strands into a bowl. The fork will help with the creation of the strands. Add marinara sauce and combine by mixing thoroughly.

Gently mix the vegetables into the squash and sauce. Serve on a bed of romaine lettuce leaves.

Sprinkle Parmesan cheese as desired.

Makes 6 servings.

KALE, QUINOA & LENTIL STEW

Adding tahini makes this a bit creamier, but it is fine without it as well. Often, health markets have a tahini sauce or tahini dressing made of sesame seeds, EVOO, lemon juice, and garlic that can be used in place of the plain sesame paste. This can be made for dinner in 45 minutes and provides a flavorful, nourishing meal. Power packed with plant nutrients from the kale, this dish is warming and healthy!

Ingredients:

½ cup green lentils
½ cup quinoa
1 sweet or red onion, finely chopped
4 Tablespoons EVOO
1 bunch kale, de-stemmed and chopped into bite-sized pieces
2 cups potatoes (about 4 small to medium), peeled and diced
5 cups organic, low sodium vegetable broth
1 heaping teaspoon cumin
1 teaspoon curry powder
3 Tablespoons tahini
3 Tablespoons Braggs® Amino Acids Liquid Seasoning

Directions:

Heat oil in a large pot over medium heat and add onions, quinoa, and lentils. Sauté for a few minutes and add spices. Add veggie broth, potatoes, and kale and bring to a boil. Cover and turn down heat to low. Simmer for 35 to 40 minutes.

Carefully ladle half the soup from the pot into a blender or a food processor. When blended, return to pot. With this recipe only half of the stew is to be blended, this gives it a creamy yet chunky texture. Add the tahini and Braggs®, stir again until mixed well, and serve!

Makes 6 servings.

SWEET & SOUR ROASTED PINEAPPLE & BELL PEPPERS

This is a taste bud explosion! This is excellent, and it is a good way to serve vegetables to unsuspecting children. The taste is sweet, but it is offset with the lime, onion, and sesame oil. I combined it with chicken and brown rice for a very satisfying meal. Pineapples, bell peppers, and limes are all very high in vitamin C. Pineapple also contains manganese and vitamin B1, which make it great at assisting with reversing cellular damage.

Ingredients:

3 cups fresh pineapple, cubed
1 medium red bell pepper (1½ cups), cut into 1-inch cubes
1 medium red onion (1½ cups), cut into thin wedges
1 Tablespoon toasted sesame seed oil
1 Tablespoon grape seed oil
1 Tablespoon honey
1 Tablespoon unsweetened coconut flakes (optional)
1 Tablespoon lime juice
Sea salt and pepper to taste

Directions:

Preheat oven to 400°F.

Arrange pineapple cubes, red bell pepper cubes, and red onion wedges on an ungreased rimmed baking sheet. Drizzle with toasted sesame oil, grape seed oil, and honey, and season with salt and pepper, if desired. Toss to coat.

Roast pineapple mixture on center oven rack for 30 minutes or until lightly browned, turning once.

Remove from oven and sprinkle with coconut flakes, if desired, and then drizzle with lime juice.

Move mixture to a serving bowl and toss well to combine. Serve hot or at room temperature.

This can be served next to chicken or over rice—it's up to you!

Makes 6 servings.

ZUCCHINI BURGER

These make a great vegetarian meal. The chickpeas, almond meal, eggs and Greek yogurt add quite a bit of protein to this delicious burger. This can be topped with hummus, applesauce, or traditional burger toppings. Enjoy!

Ingredients:

1 15 oz can chickpeas, drained
1 cup almond meal
1 large zucchini, grated
1 small red onion, minced fine
1 egg
1 teaspoon sea salt
¼ cup grape seed oil
1 cup Greek yogurt, 2%, plain

Directions:

Purée chickpeas in a food processor until smooth. Remove from processor and stir in almond meal, zucchini, onion, egg, and salt.

Form by hand into approximately eight 4-inch patties.

In a saucepan on medium heat, add grape seed oil.

Sautee patties until golden, about 3 minutes on each side.

Makes 4 servings.

VEGETABLE LATKE

We made these with a few friends for a Hanukah party one year, they were quite a hit. This turns a boring potato latke into a vegetable variation that all guests will enjoy. On the next page, is the relish that can be used, but the traditional applesauce is just fine too.

Ingredients:

2 medium potatoes

2 carrots

2 medium zucchinis

1 cup onion, chopped

¼ cup almond meal

2 garlic cloves, minced

2 eggs, lightly beaten

Sea salt and pepper to taste

Directions:

Grate potato, carrot, zucchini; place on kitchen towel wrap and squeeze well to remove excess liquid from vegetables.

Place in a bowl and add onion, almond meal, garlic, and eggs, and salt and pepper to taste.

Coat skillet with cooking spray; heat on medium.

Spoon one well-formed patty onto skillet and cook until brown on one side and flip.

Cook until both sides brown and no liquid is coming from latke.

Makes 4 servings.

MANGO RELISH

Ingredients:

2 cups corn kernels, fresh or frozen (organic preferred)

2 Tablespoons red onion, minced

½ cup mango, chopped

½ cup fresh cilantro or parsley, chopped

½ cup fresh red bell pepper, minced

1 Tablespoon EVOO

¼ teaspoon lime juice

1 garlic clove, minced

Directions:

Combine all ingredients in a bowl and set aside. When latkes are done spoon over each one and enjoy.

VEGGIE SLICE

This is a delicious vegetable casserole and can be paired with a salad for a hearty and nutritious dinner. This is one of the few recipes in this book that contains dairy, and it is used to hold it all together as a casserole.

If you have dairy allergies, you can experiment with nut or seed cheeses. There are too many vitamins and protective compounds in this one to name, so treat yourself to a large helping of veggie slice!

Ingredients:

1 Tablespoon EVOO	2 cups carrots, grated
1 yellow onion, chopped small	2 cups swiss chard, chopped, with stalk removed
2 garlic cloves, crushed	1 cup cauliflower florets, chopped small
½ red bell pepper, diced	½ cup cooked brown rice
1 pinch cayenne (optional)	1 cup low-fat cottage cheese
2 (16 oz.) cans diced tomatoes	½ cup grated cheese
2 cups zucchini, grated	Sea salt and pepper to taste

Directions:

Preheat oven to 425°F.

Heat oil in a saucepan and add onion, garlic, red pepper, and chili, and sauté for 4 minutes or until onion is soft.

Add undrained tomatoes and simmer for 5 minutes. Add zucchini, carrots, swiss chard, and cauliflower, and simmer uncovered for 10 minutes.

Place the cooked rice and the cottage cheese in a bowl and mix well.

Add rice and cottage cheese mixture to the vegetable mixture, season with sea salt and pepper, and combine.

Transfer mixture to a large glass baking dish, and sprinkle with grated cheese. Bake for 20 minutes or until golden brown.

Serve with a salad!

Makes 6 servings.

CHAPTER 8
Healthy Entrées

All of the entrées in this section are meat-based. You will find easy and delicious preparation methods for fish, chicken, and beef. I recommend organic meats and grass-fed beef when possible.

Conventional animal-based foods contain antibiotics and hormones. When you consume conventional meats, eggs, or dairy products, those chemicals enter your body and interfere with your hormonal and digestive systems. Doing your best to consume animal products that do not contain antibiotics and hormones is important for your health.

What you will realize with the recipes in this section is that you really do not have to use a lot of ingredients to make something delicious and healthful for yourself and your families. Often, if you plan one day ahead, that is all you need to stay on track and keep the momentum going.

DUTCH OVEN CHICKEN

To make this, you need an oven-proof soup pot. I have an enamel-coated cast-iron one that gets a LOT of use in my kitchen. It has little knobs inside the lid so the vapor drips back down into the pot. This is a great way to cook chicken, and the stock and gelatin can be used later for excellent chicken soup. I either make this the night before, or I get the whole pot prepared, slide it in the oven in the early morning, and head out to the gym. By the time I get back and shower, the chicken is done!

Ingredients:

2 pounds organic chicken pieces (thighs, legs, breast meat)
1 orange, quartered with skin left on
½ teaspoon sea salt
¼ teaspoon black pepper
1 small brown onion, chopped
4 garlic cloves, chopped or crushed

Directions:

Preheat oven to 375°F.

Wash chicken and place in an ovenproof pot. Add orange, onion, garlic, and salt and pepper. Cover chicken with water, place lid on top, and put in oven. Bake for 1½ hours. It's just that simple!

Makes 6 servings.

CHICKEN MEATBALLS

These can also be made with lean grass-fed beef, buffalo, or turkey. It is best to not make them too lean as the fat adds flavor and juice, and it cooks off while baking them. Once these are made, they can be stored in your fridge and be paired with a salad for a quick meal on the go. Save yourself from burning your hands with the jalapeno by using gloves and removing the seeds to reduce the heat.

Ingredients:

2/3 pound ground chicken meat (You can use breasts, legs, and thighs. Make sure the butcher removes the skin before grinding.)

1 egg, beaten

1 cup brown basmati rice

½ cup cilantro, finely chopped

2 Tablespoons jalapenos, finely chopped (These make the dish quite spicy!)

1/3 cup green pepper, finely chopped

1/3 cup green apple, peeled and grated

1 Tablespoon crushed garlic

Directions:

In a pot, bring 2 cups of water to a boil, and add brown rice. Reduce to a simmer and cover so that just a bit of steam escapes for about 25 to 30 minutes. Rice is done when all water is absorbed and rice is tender.

Preheat oven to 375°F.

Combine all ingredients in a bowl and mix thoroughly. Drop meatball-sized blobs onto a rimmed baking tray. (They will be quite sloppy.) Bake in the oven for 15 minutes until barely done. Then turn oven on to broil for 5 to 8 minutes until tops are browned. Serve and enjoy!

Makes 4 servings.

GRILLED CHICKEN RATATOUILLE

Grilling adds amazing flavor. Get these veggies prepped and ready to grill, then make the marinade and soaking them in it. This dish can be served hot or cold and it is tasty either way. Set some aside and take it for lunch the next day. If you don't have a barbeque grill, you can use an electric George Forman Grill or check out the Weber Baby Gas Grill. Both are easy to use even for a single gal! I have a patient who packs her George Forman in her suitcase and uses it in her hotel room. Now that's commitment!

Ingredients:

3 Tablespoons EVOO
3 Tablespoons fresh basil, chopped
1 Tablespoon fresh marjoram, chopped
1 teaspoon sea salt
Canola or EVOO cooking spray
1 red bell pepper; halved lengthwise, stemmed, and seeded
1 small eggplant, cut into half-inch rounds
1 medium zucchini, halved lengthwise
4 plum tomatoes, halved lengthwise
1 medium red onion, cut into half-inch rounds
4 boneless, skinless chicken breasts (about 1¼ pound)
¼ teaspoon pepper, freshly ground
1 Tablespoon red wine vinegar

Ratatouille Directions:

Preheat grill to medium-high.

Combine EVOO, basil, marjoram, and salt in a small bowl, and reserve 1 Tablespoon of the mixture in another small bowl. Set aside.

Marinate the vegetables, (bell pepper, eggplant, zucchini, tomato, and onion pieces) in the oil and herb mixture, until well coated. Grill the vegetables, turning once, until soft and charred in spots – about

5 minutes per side for the pepper, 4 minutes per side for the eggplant and zucchini, and 3 minutes per side for the tomatoes and onion. As the vegetables finish cooking, place them in a large bowl. Cover the bowl with plastic wrap.

Grilled Chicken Directions:

Rub the Tablespoon of reserved herb mixture on both sides of chicken and sprinkle with pepper. Grill the chicken until cooked through and no longer pink in the center (about 4 to 5 minutes per side).

Transfer the grilled vegetables to a cutting board and chop into 1-inch pieces. Serve the grilled chicken with the ratatouille.

Makes 6 servings.

SIMPLE FISH

Fish can be prepared and cooked in a flash! Here is an easy recipe that is light and tasty. For more flavor, blend up a batch of the basic lime and honey dressing in the salad section and drizzle it over the fish before you serve it.

Ingredients:

1 pound white fish (e.g. Chilean sea bass, halibut, Dover sole, etc.)
1 pinch sea salt
1 pinch chili powder
1 pinch black pepper
Lemon wedges

Directions:

Preheat oven to 425°F.

Place fish on a rimmed baking sheet. Sprinkle with salt, pepper, and chili powder.

Bake in oven for 10 minutes per inch thickness of fish.

Add a squeeze of lemon just before you serve it.

Makes 4 servings.

EASY FLAVORFUL CHICKEN BREASTS

This is a simple way to cook chicken that can be added to salads, sides, soups or eaten sliced all by itself. It's a good idea to have some chicken cooked in your fridge for those times when you are starving and have nothing ready for dinner. Once cooked, it can be paired with a single vegetable or a salad and an entire meal can be prepared in a flash!

Ingredients:

2 organic chicken breasts, washed and rinsed
¼ cup EVOO
2 garlic cloves, crushed
½ teaspoon dried thyme
½ teaspoon dried basil
¼ teaspoon sea salt
¼ teaspoon chili powder

Directions:

Preheat oven to 350°F.

Place chicken on a large cutting board and filet in half, as if you were slicing a bagel. (This means that each breast will now turn into 2, exactly the same size but thinner portions of itself.) You should now have 4 slices of chicken breast.

In a bowl combine oil, herbs, and salt. Mix well. Rub the chicken breasts with this mixture on both sides. Place the chicken in a baking dish and put in oven to bake 10 minutes on each side. At the end of 20 minutes, turn the oven to broil and toast the top of them. This makes the herbs more flavorful.

Ensure chicken is not pink in middle and is cooked through. If you overcook the chicken, it will be dry.

Makes 6 servings.

SLOW COOKER RIBS

This recipe is great for a busy workday. Just get it all prepped in the Crock-Pot the night before and the morning before you leave the house, plug it in and set it to low. Go to work, and when you come home, you have a delicious pot of ribs that can be paired with a salad, rice, sweet potato, or steamed vegetables. Ta-da!

Ingredients:

8 beef short ribs

1 brown onion, sliced

2 Tablespoons coarse spicy ground mustard with seeds (I recommend Plochman's.)

2 Tablespoons fresh garlic, crushed

½ teaspoon sea salt

Directions:

Add onions to bottom of a Dutch oven or Crock-Pot. In a small bowl combine the garlic, mustard, and salt. Smear ribs with garlic, mustard, and salt combination. Place ribs in the Dutch oven or Crock-Pot and add water to cover the ribs.

If you're using a Crock-Pot, cook on low for 8 to 11 hours. If you're using a Dutch oven, cook at 225°F for 8 hours.

Ribs are done when they are falling off the bone.

Use a slotted spoon to remove ribs and a fine mesh strainer to strain the liquid for homemade beef stock to be frozen for later.

Makes 2 servings.

TURKEY CHILI

From beginning to end, this takes about forty minutes and is a great meal. I usually make up a pot of this on a Sunday or Wednesday, and it helps get me through lunch for the rest of the week. I put it over spinach or just eat it alone out of the bowl. It's great for breakfast too! This can be made with lean grass-fed beef or buffalo as well.

Ingredients:

2 pounds ground turkey
1 large brown onion, diced small
5 garlic cloves, crushed
2 Tablespoon EVOO
½ cup green beans, chopped into half-inch pieces
½ cup frozen corn
1 small tomato, diced
1 (15 oz.) can black beans (optional)
4 leaves romaine lettuce, chopped
1 chili or taco seasoning packet from Simply Organic (Make sure that the one you purchase does not have added chemicals or MSG.)
2 Tablespoons Parmesan cheese (optional)

Directions:

In a large soup pot on medium-high heat, add EVOO, tomato, onion, and garlic. Sauté for about 5 minutes. Then add ground turkey and stir repeatedly to chop into small pieces. Cook thoroughly for about 10 minutes.

Put chili seasoning packet into a measuring cup and add ¾ cup warm water. Stir until combined. Pour seasoning mixture over turkey and add black beans, corn, and green beans. Cook for about 15 minutes to combine flavors and cook through.

When ready to serve, place in a bowl and sprinkle Parmesan and chopped romaine on top. Enjoy!

Makes 6 servings.

SHREDDED CHICKEN TACO STEW

This dish is a weekly staple in a busy house. With minimal effort this healthy dish cooks itself. Just put it all in a Crock-Pot®, set it on low and go to work, school, soccer, or wherever. For carbohydrate conscious moms, this can be served over shredded lettuce, and for a house of hungry growing men it can be served with corn tortillas or rice.

Ingredients:

1 medium brown onion, chopped

1 (16 oz.) can black beans, rinsed and drained

1 (16 oz.) can red kidney beans, rinsed and drained

$1/3$ cup water

2 cups frozen organic corn

1 (8 oz.) can tomato sauce

2 medium tomatoes, diced

1 packet "Simply Organic" brand taco seasoning mix

2 boneless skinless organic chicken breasts

$1/2$ cup fresh cilantro, chopped

Directions:

Add all ingredients to Crock-Pot® or Dutch oven, except chicken and cilantro. Mix well. Lay chicken breasts on top of ingredients and cover. Cook on low for 6 to 8 hours or high for 3 to 4 hours. Before serving, shred chicken, add cilantro and return to slow cooker and stir.

Ready to serve with a salad!

Makes 4 servings.

CRUNCHY WHITE FISH

I got this recipe from one of my patients, and it is a great alternative to unhealthy, gluten battered fried fish.

White fish can refer to halibut, cod, flounder or sole. This is a good way to introduce children to fish; a little batter goes a long way. A great accompaniment is the sweet potato fries found in the sides chapter of this book. Go ahead and give it a whirl!

Ingredients:

½ cup almond meal
½ cup rice flour
½ cup coconut flakes dried, unsweetened
2 Tablespoons EVOO
¼ cup fresh parsley, chopped
2 teaspoons lemon zest, grated
1 teaspoon sea salt
1 pound white fish (4 oz. each = 4 pieces)
32 oz. baby spinach (4 cups)

Directions:

Preheat oven to 400°F.
Combine almond meal, rice flour, coconut, EVOO, parsley, lemon zest and salt in a medium bowl.
Rinse fish under water and pat dry.
Press fish into batter and coat thoroughly.
Transfer fish to a rimmed baking sheet. (For crunchy fish both front and back, place a wire rack in the baking sheet so oven air will circulate around the fish while it is cooking.)
Bake for about 14 minutes.
In a medium sauce pan on medium heat add ¼ cup water and spinach, sprinkle with ¼ tsp sea salt. Cover and gently wilt spinach until bright green, about 1 to 2 minutes.
Transfer to plates and add fish.

Makes 4 servings.

JUICY TURKEY BURGERS

Tired of dry, tasteless turkey burgers? This recipe is fantastic! For years I stayed away from turkey burgers because of that dry cardboard taste but in this recipe the eggs add moisture, and the herb combination adds a LOT of flavor. I served with a salad, wild rice, grilled onions, spicy brown mustard and hot sauce on the burger. Mmmm good.

Ingredients:

3 pounds lean ground turkey
½ cup fresh cilantro, chopped
½ cup fresh parsley, chopped
½ cup fresh scallions (green onions), chopped
2 eggs
½ teaspoon sea salt
½ teaspoon black pepper
1 teaspoon crushed red pepper

Directions:

Mix all ingredients thoroughly and form into burger patties. This recipe makes six half pound burgers. Place on pre-heated grill and cook for 7 to 9 minutes on each side. Make sure the burger is cooked through before removing from heat.

Makes 6 servings.

YELLOW & RED STUFFED PEPPERS

As a kid I really disliked stuffed peppers. They were made with green peppers, ground beef and tomato sauce. This combination resulted in a bitter acidic flavor. I guarantee that this recipe is nothing like that.

Use the red, yellow, or orange peppers, it makes a BIG difference, and adds sweetness to the recipe. The key is to have the brown rice cooked ahead of time, and then this recipe is a cinch. This can be made with ground turkey, or chicken sausage. The Parmesan is optional.

Ingredients:

1 ½ teaspoons EVOO

1 pound sweet chicken sausage (Italian style)

1 zucchini, diced small

1 medium yellow onion, diced

1 garlic clove, minced

4 cups brown rice, cooked

¼ cup Parmesan, grated (optional)

½ cup almond meal

¼ teaspoon sea salt and black pepper

4 large bell peppers halved lengthwise, seeds and ribs removed

Directions:

Preheat oven to 400°F.

In a large skillet heat EVOO and add onion and garlic. Cook on medium-high for 5 minutes. Squeeze chicken sausage from casing and add to sauce pan, breaking up meat as it cooks with a spatula or spoon. Once meat is half cooked, add zucchini, salt and pepper. When fully cooked, transfer to a bowl and add cooked rice, almond meal, and Parmesan, and mix well.

Spoon mixture into peppers and set in glass baking dish with open sides up. Add 2/3 cup water to bottom of dish to prevent sticking.

Bake until peppers are soft and stuffing is brown, about 30 minutes.

Makes 6 servings.

CHAPTER 9
Healthy Desserts

I recently saw an advertisement for a gluten-free cookbook with a giant chocolate cake on the front cover. Just because something is gluten-free doesn't mean it is good for you. Gluten-free baking, if not done healthfully, contains refined sugars and grains.

Be a savvy shopper; don't be fooled by "gluten-free" labeling. Know the difference between real food and processed food disguised as health food.

Cooking is one thing and baking is another. It is much more difficult to bake something healthy than it is to cook something healthy. This is true because baking typically requires yeast, refined grains, gluten, and sugars in order to get it to stick together and look pretty. This presents a dilemma for those of us interested in providing healthy desserts.

I often hear, "I want to make dessert because I'm having company over. What can I make that is on my plan that my guests can enjoy too?"

The answer is that the key to healthy baking is avoiding the refined sugars and grains, and increasing the fiber, protein, and nutrients. This section provides exactly that- healthy desserts that can be eaten as snacks or after a delicious meal. In fact, they are so nutritious that they may even make a better breakfast than most standard American breakfast options.

When baking gluten-free, things tend to be less moist, because of the lack of gluten. Using mashed banana, applesauce, soaked flax seeds, and yogurt, helps bring moisture to gluten-free baked goods. Any kind of baking takes time, so with some of these recipes, you might want to double them up and store the muffins or cookies in the freezer for a later time.

There are three recipes in this section that call for oats. If you are sensitive to gluten or have celiac disease then you must choose gluten-free oats. Oats can sometimes be contaminated with gluten depending on where they are grown. A good oat substitute in cookies is cooked brown or wild rice. Simply cook the rice, let it cool, chop it in a food processor, and add it in place of oats.

ALMOND BUTTER BITES

This recipe makes about two dozen, but you had better double it and freeze them for later – because these bites are delicious and packed with protein. These are a great finger dessert for a party and equally good to pack on a hike. Almond butter is milder than peanut butter, and it blends well with the other flavors. I prefer currants because they are a bit smaller than raisins.

Ingredients:

2½ cups gluten-free rolled oats
½ cup raw pumpkin seeds (These are also known as pepitas.)
½ cup raisins or currants
2 Tablespoons raw sunflower seeds
1 teaspoon cinnamon
½ cup almond butter
⅓ cup plus 1 Tablespoon honey
1 Tablespoon agave syrup
1 teaspoon vanilla extract

Directions:

Grind ½ cup gluten-free oats and ¼ cup pumpkin seeds in food processor until powdery. Transfer to a medium bowl and set aside.

Combine remaining 2 cups gluten-free oats, remaining ¼ cup pumpkin seeds, raisins or currants, sunflower seeds, and cinnamon in a large bowl. Stir in almond butter, honey, agave syrup, and vanilla until soft dough forms.

Moisten hands and roll dough into 1-inch balls. Coat balls in oat-pumpkin seed powder. Place in freezer on a cookie sheet for 20 minutes to set and then serve or store in the refrigerator.

Makes 12 servings.

REFRESHING ANTIOXIDANT PIE

You're never going to believe it, but this is truly a healthy pie. The unhealthy part is the crust. You can choose to make a gluten-free crust or avoid it all together by putting the filling in little dessert cups and serving it that way.

The berries are packed with nutrients, bioflavinoids, and antioxidants. Health benefits include improving circulation to the eye and brain, strengthening vessels, and decreasing inflammation just to name a few. I usually make two pies at one time. It takes exactly the same amount of time to make one or two, so use your time wisely.

Ingredients:

2½ cups fresh blackberries or blueberries, rinsed and patted dry
1 pound bag frozen blueberries or other dark berries, such as a berry blend
⅓ cup agave sweetener
1 teaspoon cinnamon
1 teaspoon lemon zest
3 Tablespoons cornstarch
1 to 2 gluten-free pie shells

Directions:

Preheat the oven to 350°F.

Prick the pie shell with a fork to prevent steam from getting caught underneath it. Precook it for about 20 minutes in the oven until golden brown, remove, and set aside to cool. Once cooled, add fresh berries to cooked pie shell.

In a saucepan on medium heat, add ¼ cup water and thawed frozen berries. Mix in agave, cinnamon, and lemon zest. Combine well. Add in cornstarch and stir slowly until thick. Remove from heat, and pour cooked berry mixture on top of fresh berries in pie shell. Place in refrigerator to cool.

Makes 8 servings.

BASIC MUFFIN RECIPE

This is a gluten- and dairy-free baking combination that can be adapted to your muffin of choice. It's extremely versatile and a healthier option than most traditional after-school snacks. These can be used as a breakfast replacement for a nutritious way to start the day. This recipe makes about twelve muffins and they can be frozen for later.

Muffin Batter Ingredients:

½ cup ground golden flaxseeds soaked in ½ cup water overnight or for at least 30 minutes. (This is the egg substitute.)
¾ cup grape seed oil or butter
¾ cup brown sugar or agave
2 teaspoons baking powder
¾ cup corn meal
½ cup ground almond meal
½ cup gluten-free oats or quinoa flour
½ cup rice or almond milk as needed (Add if batter is too thick.)

Blueberry Almond Muffin Ingredients:

1 teaspoon almond extract
¾ cup frozen blueberries

Lemon Poppy Seed Muffin Ingredients:

1 teaspoon lemon extract
1 Tablespoon lemon zest
¼ cup poppy seeds

Orange Cranberry Muffin Ingredients:

½ cup orange juice in place of milk
1 Tablespoon orange zest
1 teaspoon orange extract
½ cup cranberries (If you can find orange-flavored cranberries, that's even better.)

Directions:

Preheat oven to 350°F.

Mix all batter ingredients together in a bowl. Combine batter with chosen add-in ingredients from the list above.

Place paper muffin cups in a muffin or cupcake tin. Fill muffin cups halfway with batter and cook 20 to 25 minutes or until an inserted toothpick comes out clean.

Makes 12 muffins.

HEALTHY FUDGE CAKE

If you don't tell them, they will never know that this is made with black beans! This delicious little treat is grain-free and filled with fiber and antioxidants—a perfect complement to a meal after dinner or special occasion. It is incredibly moist and guests will be coming back for seconds.

Ingredients:

Olive oil or non-stick cooking spray
4 ounces dark organic chocolate
1½ cup cooked black beans, rinsed and drained
2 eggs
1 egg white
2 Tablespoons EVOO
¼ cup unsweetened cocoa powder
1 teaspoon baking powder
¼ cup unsweetened applesauce
½ cup raw walnuts, chopped
1 teaspoon vanilla extract
½ cup agave syrup

Directions:

Preheat oven to 350°F.

Grease a 9-inch round pie pan with cooking spray.

Melt dark chocolate in a small saucepan with 1 Tablespoon water.

Combine melted chocolate, beans, eggs, egg white, oil, cocoa powder, baking powder, vanilla, applesauce, and agave in a food processor. Blend until smooth. Stir in walnuts and pour into a greased baking dish.

Bake in oven until top is dry and edges start to pull away from the sides (about 30 minutes).

Makes 8 servings.

OATMEAL HARVEST COOKIES

These are so healthy they can be eaten for breakfast! Make a double batch and freeze these cookies for later.

Ingredients:

½ cup grape seed oil
25 drops vanilla flavored liquid stevia
1 egg or 2 Tablespoons whole flaxseeds, soaked for 30 minutes in ¼ cup water
1 teaspoon vanilla extract
¼ cup unsweetened almond milk
¼ cup unsweetened applesauce
1 cup garbanzo flour or brown rice flour
½ teaspoon baking soda
½ teaspoon cinnamon
¼ teaspoon sea salt
¼ teaspoon nutmeg
1¼ cups gluten free oats
½ cup raisins, ¼ cup cranberries, or ½ cup chocolate chips
½ cup chopped walnuts (optional)

Directions:

Preheat oven to 375°F.

In a large bowl, cream together oil, stevia, egg or flax seeds, applesauce, almond milk, and vanilla extract.

In a saucepan on medium heat, toast the walnuts, stirring regularly for about 7 minutes and set aside.

In a separate bowl, combine the flour, oats, baking soda, salt, and spices. Fold into the liquid mixture and mix well. Fold in raisins, nuts, and cranberries. Drop Tablespoons 2 inches apart onto a baking sheet and flatten with fingers.

Bake about 12 minutes or until lightly browned. Set aside to cool.

Makes 18 cookies.

POACHED PEARS WITH ORANGE JUICE

Pears are rich in vitamin C, calcium, and magnesium, and the presence of fiber in pears helps to prevent constipation and ensure digestive regularity in general. Additionally, pears are a hypoallergenic fruit, and the high content of pectin in pears makes them useful in lowering cholesterol levels.

One orange can supply up to 60 percent of the daily requirement of vitamin C, so eat up these delectable and juicy slices!

Ingredients:

4 firm ripe pears
½ teaspoon orange extract
5 drops liquid stevia (orange flavor optional)
⅓ cup fresh squeezed orange juice
¼ cup water
1 to 2 teaspoons grated orange zest

Directions:

Peel pears, cut in halves or quarters, and cut out cores. In a saucepan, heat the stevia, orange juice, and water over medium heat. Add the pears and bring to a simmer. Reduce heat to low, cover, and continue simmering for 15 minutes or until the pears are tender. Remove pears from the saucepan and add the orange zest to the remaining syrup. Simmer the syrup for 5 minutes longer, then combine the pears and syrup and chill thoroughly.

Makes 8 servings.

OLD-FASHIONED BROWN RICE PUDDING

I never could understand why traditional rice pudding wasn't made with brown rice. Well now, I have created my own healthy version with more fiber, less sugar, and less guilt!

This is a drier variety of the typical runny rice pudding, but this one is packed with protein. It is delicious hot or cold. Because the hull of the rice remains, brown rice brings more nutrients and fiber into this dish. Cooking the brown rice in the almond milk instead of water makes it a bit creamier.

The currants are little juicy bombs of flavor that really add to this dish. If you have a dairy sensitivity, you can leave out the Greek yogurt, and it will be a bit more crumbly.

Ingredients:

$1^{2}/_{3}$ cups water or unsweetened almond milk
$^{2}/_{3}$ cup uncooked basmati brown rice
2 eggs
10 to 12 drops liquid stevia, vanilla flavored
$^{1}/_{4}$ teaspoon sea salt
$^{3}/_{4}$ cup unsweetened almond milk
1 cup Greek yogurt
$^{1}/_{3}$ cup currants (optional)
$^{1}/_{2}$ teaspoon nutmeg
$^{1}/_{2}$ teaspoon cinnamon

Directions:

In a medium pot, bring water or almond milk to boil and stir in rice. Cover and reduce heat. Simmer until rice is tender and all liquid is absorbed (about 35 minutes).
Preheat oven to 350°F.

In a large bowl, beat together eggs, stevia, salt, and milk. Stir in yogurt and add hot rice and currants if desired. Pour into 9 inch round glass baking dish and sprinkle with nutmeg and cinnamon. Cover and bake 30 minutes or until barely set. Bake uncovered 10 minutes before removing from oven.

Makes 4 servings.

ROSEMARY SHORTBREAD COOKIE

"Oh, wow!" That's what my husband said when he tried these. These cookies are a buttery short-bread cookie without the shortbread.

Rosemary has been used for enhancing memory for centuries. I clipped a 3-inch stalk from my plant and removed the aromatic leaves from the stems and put them in my mini coffee grinder; they chopped nicely. These cookies are perfect with tea and are highly addictive!

Ingredients:

1 ¼ cups blanched almond flour

¼ teaspoon sea salt

¼ teaspoon baking soda

¼ cup grape seed oil

2 Tablespoons agave nectar

1 teaspoon vanilla extract

1 Tablespoon fresh rosemary, minced

½ cup pecans, finely chopped

Directions:

Preheat oven to 350°F. In a medium bowl, combine almond flour, salt, rosemary, pecans and baking soda. In a small bowl, whisk together oil, agave, and vanilla. Mix wet ingredients into dry.

Form dough into ½- to 1-inch balls and press onto prepared baking sheet. (If batter gets sticky, wet hands before forming cookies.) Bake for 6 to 7 minutes, until golden. Cool on baking sheet.

Makes 20 cookies.

HEALTHY CHOCOLATE PUDDING

Not only is this pudding dairy-free, but it is raw as well. With a base of avocado, this pudding satisfies for hours, with just the right balance of protein and healthy fat.

I have made this without a food processor, just use a potato masher instead. This is best when thoroughly chilled, and sprinkled with sea salt before serving.

Ingredients:

3 avocados
6 Tablespoons cocoa powder
¼ cup honey
1 teaspoon vanilla extract
1/8 teaspoon sea salt

Directions:

Purée avocados, cocoa powder, honey, and vanilla in food processor until smooth.

Sprinkle with salt before serving.

Makes 4 servings.

THANKSGIVING PUDDING

This pudding reminds me of a dessert that was made in the 1700's, and I was tempted to call it Homestead Pudding. It is rustic with the cornmeal and puréed butternut squash, and has a sweet taste with a grainy texture. I cooked it in a glass pie shell but it can be poured into individual ramekins and baked. It can be served with non-dairy ice cream to guests, and they will never guess it has squash in it!

Ingredients:

1 small to medium butternut squash

2 cups almond milk

½ cup cornmeal, organic preferred

½ teaspoon cinnamon, ground

½ teaspoon ginger, ground

½ teaspoon pumpkin pie spice

½ teaspoon sea salt

1 Tablespoon butter or coconut oil

2 Tablespoons molasses, unsulphured

25 drops liquid stevia, vanilla flavored

Directions:

Preheat oven to 350°F.

Slice butternut squash lengthwise and scoop out seeds. Place cut side down on baking sheet and cook in oven for 45 minutes or until a knife inserted passes through cleanly. Remove squash from oven, reduce heat to 300°F.

Set squash aside to cool for 15 minutes, then scoop flesh from skin and mash in a bowl with a potato masher. When well mashed, add molasses and stevia; mix well.

Coat glass pie shell with butter or coconut oil.

In a saucepan whisk almond milk, cornmeal, cinnamon, pumpkin pie spice, ginger and salt. Cook for 15 minutes and whisk again to combine all ingredients. This will thicken; remove from heat and stir in butter. Combine with squash mixture, and pour into pie shell. Bake uncovered for 1 hour, or until toothpick comes out clean.

Serve with coconut milk vanilla ice cream.

Makes 6 servings.

CONCLUSION

Although this book is ending, it is only the beginning of your nutritional journey. It is crucial to know what to eat for your immediate performance and stamina and for your long-term health. Eating well prevents disease, and it keeps your body running efficiently and detoxifying properly. Without both of those things, our bodies become clogged over time, just like a filter.

This is a beginning for you to use these recipes and integrate healthy food into your daily routine. This should be a platform from which to understand healthy ingredient substitutes and make better choices in some of your own family recipes.

Some of the most important foods that both nourish and detoxify are the dark green leafy vegetables and the cruciferous vegetable family (such as broccoli, cauliflower, radishes, cabbage, brussels sprouts, and kale). Make these vegetables a part of your weekly shopping list.

Get started preparing nutritious food for yourself and your family.

You're worth it!

INTERNET RESOURCES

American Association of
Naturopathic Physicians
www.Naturopathic.org
Find an Integrated Naturopathic
Physician in your area.

Find Dr. Purcell Online
www.AskDrPurcell.com

Have a health-related question?
www.AskDrPurcell.com

All-Clad
www.All-Clad.com
Stainless steel cookware

Le Creuset
www.LeCreuset.com
Enamel Dutch ovens and stoneware

Lodge Cast Iron
www.LodgeMFG.com
Cast-iron cookware

You can also check out the cooking tips on **www.AskDrPurcell.com** to find out how to season a cast-iron pan, as well as more recipes!

You can also find Dr. Purcell online at these social networking websites:

facebook.   **twitter**   **You Tube**   **Linked in.**

http://Facebook.com/DrAndreaPurcell

http://Twitter.com/AskDrPurcell

http://YouTube.com/DrAndreaPurcell

http://LinkedIn.com/in/DrAndreaPurcell

ABOUT THE AUTHOR

Dr. Purcell is licensed as a primary care physician in California and Arizona. She received her doctorate in naturopathic medicine from Southwest College of Naturopathic Medicine and earned her BS in environmental science from the University of Massachusetts Amherst.

Dr. Purcell has helped thousands of people regain their health and vitality through natural medicine and nutrition during her ten years of bicoastal private practice. She is an expert in medical nutrition and recommends food selections based on each patient's individual needs. She is adamant about educating people about prevention and proactive health care.

Dr. Purcell believes that what we eat is at the core of our health. From that point, we can either gain health or fall into disease. Dr. Purcell combines the therapies of nutrition, natural hormone balancing, herbs, homeopathy, nutritional supplementation, and vitamin therapy to restore her patients to optimal health.

58796092R00082

Made in the USA
Middletown, DE
08 August 2019